Surviving Domestic Violence

A work of fiction for those who chose to walk the path
of the abuser and a work of fact for those who found
themselves unwillingly walking the path of the abused...

by

Lily Anne Burnett

PublishAmerica
Baltimore

First printing

PublishAmerica has allowed this work to remain exactly as the author intended, verbatim, without editorial input.

Hardcover 978-1-4512-0230-4
Softcover 978-1-4512-0252-6
PUBLISHED BY PUBLISHAMERICA, LLLP
www.publishamerica.com
Baltimore

Printed in the United States of America

Dedicated to:

I dedicate this book to all my gal pals who helped me stay afloat while I navigated the stormy waters of abuse, infidelity, and ultimately divorce. I'd also like to thank the handful of men in my life who gave me unconditional love and support. A special thanks, and much love, goes to my two knights in shining armor and my saving grace; Mom loves you!

Acknowledgment:

When I began writing this book I thought I would be going through all of it alone. I was diving head first into a sea of painful memories with no safety line. When I knew this work of mine was going to be something I wanted others to read, I looked to an old friend of mine for support and feedback. He was the right choice to be the first one to read what I had gone through for so many years, and I am glad to call him my friend. Thanks for all your support and uplifting words that kept me going…

I'd also like to thank my Aunt Sue and Uncle Steve for providing me a safe haven to retreat to when I felt the ghosts of my past would consume me. Being out there with you both recharged my mental battery and reconfirmed in my soul that love is not lost in this world…

PREFACE

I am going to make it clear right now that this book of mine is not pretty, full of roses and rainbows, or drowning in happy memories of a perfect life. This is a book about my first marriage; my thirteen plus years in a very violent relationship. I spent all those years feeling utterly alone and I believe no woman should go through that kind of pain alone. I am only warning you of this now to give you the opportunity to put this book back on the shelf you took it from. I will have my moments when I will cuss at the page as though it were my abuser, I will rage against all the wrongs put upon me by another, I will not be politically correct to some folks reading this… This book is me and I am raw. I refuse to hold back anything just because it may offend someone. I am writing the truth. I am writing how I feel. I am letting it out and letting it go. If that is too much for you, then by all means put the book back. If you are a victim of domestic violence though, or know anyone who is, I strongly encourage you to read on…

Those of us who make it through the battlefields of abuse all feel the same way, that we are all alone in our struggles, but I am about to prove you wrong. No matter if you are twenty or sixty-five; you're not alone. No matter what your nationality or ethnicity; you're not alone. No matter if you are married, divorced, engaged, or engaged to be engaged; you're not alone. No matter if you have children or are childless; you're not alone. No matter if you have a college degree or never graduated high school; you're not alone. No matter if you are Catholic, Jewish, Muslim, Agnostic or Atheist; you're not alone. No matter if you call it domestic violence, domestic abuse, wife beating, intimate partner abuse, or "I slipped and fell"; you're not alone. About one-third of abuse is reported each year and the odds are, if you are reading this, you are among those of us who didn't report it. Don't feel bad; you're not alone.

For thirteen years I thought I was alone; that everything was my fault; that my marriage would change; that I could have the whole fairy tale. Well, I finally came to the realization that I was not alone; that everything wasn't my fault; that my marriage would never change; that the fairy tale I wanted was never going to come true. It was a hard pill to swallow when I came to that realization, but I know I am not the only one to swallow that bitter pill of reality. Throughout these pages I will keep reminding you that you're not alone. Some days you will feel that is true and some days, sadly, you won't. On the days you feel it isn't true I hope you flip through the pages of this book and remember you're not alone; you're never alone; you don't have to go through all this mess alone. I am here and every single woman who is going through the same Hell as you, or is trying to leave it behind, is here too. So, grab a snack, box of tissues, and curl up on the couch, recliner, porch swing, or bed and read a few pages from a woman who can safely say, "you're not alone."

I'm not really sure when I started this epic journey of trying to write about my life. What I do know is I have been typing only to delete, only to type and delete again for what seems like ages. I must admit it was a vicious cycle that I thought I would never get out of. I came to the conclusion I was going about chronicling my life all wrong. Here I was, day after day and night after night, trying to put my life; my feelings; my pain; my sorrow; my self-proclaimed wisdom; my happiness into neat little chapters. My overwhelming need for perfection and control only led me into not accomplishing what I knew I needed, or should I say had, to do. I needed to write about my life, all aspects of it, whether it was good or bad. You can't put your life into nice neat chapters; no one's life is perfect.

So, now I start my attempts at writing about my life with a new outlook... No chapters, no thirst for perfection, no rules; just me and what I feel and think. Hell, I doubt I will even have the punctuation right half the time. I never liked English grammar and therefore never retained much of what I had to learn throughout my academic years. I think what I write should be left with its flaws, its imperfections. You don't have any objection to a misused comma or semi-colon do you? All I need and desire is that you walk away from what I write on these pages with a better sense of self-worth and appreciation for life. I don't think that is asking too much. Though I suppose if anyone gets the privilege of editing my writing, they will probably have their work cut out for them.

So, why did I begin this work in the first place? I started it as a form of therapy for myself and any woman who has felt utterly alone at any point in her life. I started this book (so loosely called) because I spent over thirteen years in an abusive relationship, only to be kicked out and forced to leave my three amazingly beautiful children behind. Okay, how many women read that last part and began calling me every nasty name in the known languages of the world for "leaving my children"? Well, read again the words prior to my admittance of having to leave my children and you will begin to understand my position and state of mind at the time. Oh, don't worry, I will explain more as I go along. First though, before I start to ramble about nothing in particular, let me give you a rough idea of who I am and who I am not. It will be a brief synopsis of both though for now. I just don't want you wondering about the basics as you read on.

Who am I? You have no idea how many times over the past thirteen plus years I have asked myself that very same question. Before I go on and on about the universal concept of who I am today let me give you some simple facts. I am a thirty-seven year old mother of three beautiful children. I married my second husband in 2007 and he has a son, which makes me a step-mom, though I am still trying to figure out how to fill that role properly. I was born in Michigan, but do not feel it is my "home state". When I was shy of turning twenty-one I met my first husband while attending college in Northern Michigan. Over the course of the following thirteen years I got married, gave birth three times, became a victim of domestic violence, moved from place to place; state to state, went completely blind from an eye disease, was cheated on, kicked out of my so-called home, was forced to leave my children, got divorced, and surprisingly managed to recover from most of that drama... Now that, I have to admit, was a mouthful! But, now that you have a general idea of my life history up to this point let me share with you who I am not. I am not a shrink; I am not a certified counselor; I am not a licensed therapist; I am not a pastor or priest or rabbi. I am you… I am you and you are me and we are just in different stages of our journey right now. What journey you ask? The journey that leads us back to the vibrant woman we were before being beaten down, yelled at, torn apart, and left for dead; dead emotionally, spiritually, mentally, and a slap away from physically. Let us take a moment to thank whatever higher power we believe in for allowing us to see the light of another day.

The longer I sit here at my computer I begin to realize it is much easier to say who I was before all the name calling and hitting and hair pulling and pushing and shouting began, and who I am now after ridding myself of it. We'll get to who I truly am later on. For now let's talk about who I was prior to the years, I felt, were a prison sentence full of nothing but torment, loneliness, and doubt. Thirteen years of torment dished out by the very man who professed to love me; loneliness because I felt I would never have a true friend or my family in my life; doubt that I would ever see the proverbial light at the end of the tunnel. I was the youngest of three children; a sister, daughter, and granddaughter. I was taught by my grandmother how to draw, paint, creatively write, and yodel. My grandfather taught me to never ever put blue berries in your pocket (leaves a nasty stain), how to drive a tractor and snowmobile, how to change a tire, and to drink coffee with caution because the first sip is "going to be hot". Growing up I attended the local Methodist church on my own. I became a member of the choir and youth group. As I got older I joined the choir in school, became captain of our school's flag corps, and a peer counselor. All that I wanted in life lie before me with nothing to stand in my way. I spent every summer possible with my grandparents, lying on the beach for hours, painting, walking through the woods; basically soul searching. I was so incredibly lucky to have had those summers with my grandparents. My grandmother taught me to respect nature and understand that every living thing from the tiniest of insects to the ugliest of human beings holds a purpose in our lives. My grandfather taught me that what we gain through hard work and perseverance was greater by far than anything handed to us on a silver platter. They both taught me to always hold my head high and be proud of who I am; no matter what.

Somewhere between the name calling and fits of slaps, punches, and kicks from my first husband those lessons got lost though and I became someone unrecognizable by myself, my family, and my friends. It is amazing how years of love and praise can be wiped clean from our memory by one simple act of cruelty. For me, that one simple act of cruelty by the hands of my first husband didn't stop there; it lasted for thirteen plus years. I am not proud of what I allowed to become of myself during my pathetic excuse of a first marriage. I often wondered where the hell my backbone disappeared to. One minute I was standing on my own two feet, waiting to take on the world, and the next minute I was being held up by the invisible noose around my neck courtesy of my first husband.

Please tell me what happens to us ladies between the ages of sixteen and twenty-three that makes us believe we "know" what true love is. 'Cause let's face it; we don't. It is like some chemical imbalance takes place and we are blinded by what is really going on. Our first love isn't Prince Charming; he is the Devil, he is the wolf in sheep's clothing... Oh yeah, he is sweet, kind, attentive, caring, etc at first. He is all those things long enough to suck you in, then you wake up to either a verbal slapping or physical pistol whipping thinking, "How the hell did I get here and who am I and who is that guy?" I kid you not, thousands of women go through this disgusting "rite of passage". Why can't our rite of passage be something a little less damaging to our self-worth and mental stability? Why do so many of us women feel we deserve a good beatin' before we can stand proud? You think guys feel they need to subject themselves to abuse for years upon years before finding their backbone? I wonder if it is in our genetic makeup... Ladies take the beating; guys dish it out... The more I think about it though I truly believe men do the beating and name calling because they couldn't take being on the receiving end of all of it. Men aren't as strong or resilient as us women are... Ever notice that? Yes, I realize I am ranting, but this is my show and I don't care that I am ranting and not following the "rules of writing". All I know for sure is I don't want my two boys turning out like their pig of a father has and that my daughter learns from my mistakes not her own.

How do I feel about my first husband today? I feel nothing, absolutely nothing. It is a fact that he is what he is and nothing more needs to be said at this point. I am confident once I relive the past throughout the following pages I will surely feel something along the lines of anger, hatred, sadness, pity, and regret. For now though; nothing. Does this make me an unfeeling bitch, no. My abuser was a controlling, manipulative, abusive monster when I was involved with him and is all those things still today. Facts are facts no matter what state of denial my first husband chooses to reside in.

Who am I now? I am a survivor, that is who I am... I am a survivor of mental abuse. I am a survivor of physical abuse. I am a survivor of the eye disease I was born with and subsequently went blind from. I am a survivor of the messed up childhood I shared with my brother and sister. I am a survivor of a marriage gone terribly wrong. I am a survivor of life's battles and who loves who she has become; scars and all. Beyond that, I am a woman that loves being a mom and newlywed. I truly love my life! Oh, don't think for one moment that I don't have my flashbacks of days gone terribly wrong because I do. Sorry, but as of yet I have not learned how to control what I dream or those things in life that spark past memories. If anyone knows a sure way never to dream about their past or keep out unwanted ghosts, short of falling into a medicated coma, please let me know.

So, we have gone over who I used to be and who I am now. Am I ready to delve into the years of my first marriage or what I like to call "lessons in what I don't want out of a real marriage"? Why yes I am. The only problem I see with this topic is that there are so many years to cover, so much pain, so much crap… Where the hell do I start? What do I talk about? What do I leave out? At least I know when I do go walking through the path of my past, I won't shed a single tear for each day I wasted on my first husband and that is really saying something!

"In the beginning…" Most of us ladies have probably started our life's story off with those exact words. But, then it is usually followed up with a slue of excuses explaining how we either got suckered in by our abuser or how he wasn't "always" that way, blah blah blah… I may sound harsh, but I have lived it, I have thought it, I have said it, I have dreaded it; all of it. Everything you ladies have felt or are feeling, so have I. I could probably fill the Grand Canyon with all the excuses I made up for my first husband's behavior; what else can you do? One of our internal defense mechanisms, which ends up being an obstacle, is us lying to ourselves about the person we thought we loved and desperately wanted to believe truly loved us in return. This being the case, here I go with my "In the Beginning"…

In the beginning my first husband was shy, understanding, fun, and protective. Wanna know what all of that turned into? Let's think back and analyze it. Shy turned out to be a ploy to gain my trust. Understanding slowly turned into judgmental. Fun turned into only being fun if it was his idea. And protective?

Oh, you ladies know damn well what "protective" turned into; jealousy and control. A lot happened during the first year I was with that... oh, I have no idea what to call him!. It was like one day I turned around to find that all my friends had vanished to be replaced by his friends. His friends that spied on me. His friends that lied about me. His friends that tried to get a little summin' summin' when my ex wasn't around or too drunk to notice. My girlfriends stayed away and my male friends would sneak a talk with me in the library or some place private like it was cloak and dagger time. And of course it didn't stop there. But, to recap; his friends were now my friends. Music? Oh, his favorite music became my favorite music and I am sorry, but I DO NOT like that older than dirt rock band you are so blessedly fond of ... Movies? What he wanted to see was what "we" wanted to see. I was slowly losing myself and becoming one of his appendages; an appendage to be seen and not heard. How many of you ladies can relate to that? See, you aren't as alone as you may feel you are.

Some of you are probably wondering to yourselves why I didn't turn hightail and run when all the warning signs were there. To be honest with you, I really have no idea what I was thinking. Maybe I was looking for a way out of my current situation; a way to free myself from an abusive childhood. I think that is what a lot of us do. We see a way out of our daily existence and stupidly believe the first creep that professes undying love really wants to give us the whole fairie tale. Those of us who grow up with a not-so-great childhood must go out into the world with a mark on our foreheads only abusive, opportunistic guys can see; or maybe they smell fresh meat to prey on. Maybe that is it...

On some deep down, cave man level, the abuser is the predator and the abused is the prey. Now, no abuser in their right mind would admit to being a "predator" and this is where the whole phrase "a work of fiction..." comes into play. Men; possibly abusive men; will read this and say, "I never did that or said that and I am definitely not a predator.", but they know deep down that they did cause all the damage we survivors finally get a backbone to talk about and they are predators. It is hard enough for those who are abused to speak out about what they allowed to happen to them. This being said, what man would EVER admit to being the one who did the abusing? Well, I suppose a changed man would; a man wanting forgiveness; a man who knows they have done wrong. I have yet to meet any man such as that though, but I digress.

The phrase "In the Beginning" keeps turning itself over and over in my head this morning. And to be honest that phrase goes a little something like this. In the beginning God created man and man turned out to be an incredible jackass!!! Now that may sound like I am some vindictive bitch who hates men, but, if I said those very same words sitting around a table with other women and drinking a great glass of wine it would seem pretty damn funny; would it not? That is the irony about all of this abuse crap. It hurts. no doubt about it, it hurts. On those rare occasions though we ladies can manage to turn tragedy into a laugh when we are in the company of those who understand, those who have gone through what we have gone through, those who have survived. And why do we do this? Simple really. We have to make a joke out of our experiences, our tragedies, our pathetic excuses of a significant other or we will go insane. Okay, maybe not literally insane, but pretty damn close to it.

How many of you ladies started drinking; no, not socially; alone? How many of you ladies stopped eating? How many of you ladies bought out the entire store and locked yourself in a room to do nothing, but eat? How many of you ladies became guilt ridden?

How many of you ladies decided not to give a damn? How many of you ladies never got your ass out of bed? How many of you ladies never put your ass to bed in order to get some seriously needed sleep? How many of you ladies cried relentlessly in the shower? How many of you ladies couldn't find the mere strength to put your smelly rear end in the shower? See, plenty of you reading this have done one or more of the aforementioned self-destructive things.

Trust me when I say I have also done a few of them. How can you not? One minute your life, though a far cry from perfect, is all you know and the next thing you find is your life has taken a completely different turn and you crumble under the weight of it all. You are not alone! I am going to keep on repeating that phrase until every last one of you reading these pages realizes that little fact… YOU ARE NOT ALONE! I have spent many o' nights in the company of JD and Sprite; you're not alone. I have gone spans of time without eating; you're not alone. I have sank into self-pity and only got out of bed to pee; you're not alone. I have gone through insomnia; you're not alone. I have found myself curled up in a ball, on the floor of the shower, crying my fool head off; you're not alone. I have gone days where I felt there was no point in taking a shower or brushing my teeth or doing anything with my hair; you're not alone. No matter what you may feel or were ever told or have had beaten into every fiber of your being; you're not alone… Not anymore.

I am pretty sure that just because you decided to pick up this book and read it; it doesn't mean that you have truly accepted you were a victim of domestic violence. So, to set you on a clear path of acknowledgement of what you went through or are still going through I am going to list the many forms of abuse and share some of what I went through at the hands of my abuser. I highly suggest you sit down for this and have a Kleenex handy.

Admitting you were abused or are currently being abused is not an easy thing to do. Just remember that I am right here with you and so is every other woman reading these very same pages. Be strong... I promise you that the pain does not last forever.

I believe it prudent to say this before I jump into the forms of abuse; what I am about to write is a necessary evil for me to endure. I am not going to like what I write, read, delete, and write again. It hurt when I lived it and it is going to hurt to relive it, but, I will do this if it means I reach at least one woman; making her realize she is not alone.

I will gladly apologize now for anything I am about to write. I am going on an emotional rollercoaster for you ladies. I will cuss like a sailor at times, I will yell at the page as if it were my abuser, I will take side roads and go off on tangents, I will cry. Oh no, they won't be tears of sadness or anger. They will be tears of triumph. I got away; I am letting go; I am learning to love myself again. It is a hard road, but something worth having is never gotten the easy way.

I also need to point out that each form of abuse runs as if it were on a scale; subtle to extreme. I don't want ladies reading this and screaming at the top of their lungs that they are a victim of domestic abuse simply because they are going through a bad bout of PMS. But, on the same note I do not want ladies to read this and minimize what they are going through...

The first form I want to discuss is incredibly subtle in the beginning, but then you wake up one morning and realize just how its roots of effectiveness run deep within your soul. This form is Emotional/Mental/Psychological Abuse. I use the term "roots of effectiveness" because even though this form of abuse is equivalent to a verbal slapping it leaves scars on your very spirit, heart, and mind that, for some of us, never go away. As with all forms of abuse this one will only escalate. It may start with a nasty name being tossed in your direction, but that nasty name eventually turns into several nasty names; ugly comments about your cooking, your appearance, your family, your friends… you name it. Your abuser will find any words necessary to bring you down and no topic is off limits. Sorry ladies, but nothing is sacred to our abusers and Emotional Abuse is where it always begins. It creeps up on you like day turning into night. Unfortunately, for some of us the night never turns back into day.

How did it start for me? Well, it is true that hind sight is 20/20 and sitting here, looking back at my life, it is easy to see that the emotional abuse was always present. It started with the name calling and threats of physical harm, went into the shouts of how worthless and lazy I was, then to how much all of my family members sucked, then into how I couldn't even hold down a job because I was so pathetic and stupid. Oh and we can't forget that I was a fat ass. I guess that must have been his pet name for me because he called me that constantly. Oh, I suppose I should give him credit for changing it up a little. It wasn't ALWAYS fat ass. It was also lazy fat ass, fucking fat ass, worthless piece of shit fat ass; get the picture? All this AND he said he loved me; hahahahahahaha!

I feel a rant coming on. Call me a lazy fat ass that can't hold a job will ya? Hey Einstein, I was fucking pregnant when I had to quit my jobs! You know; pregnant, knocked up, with child? Last I checked it takes two to get a woman in that position! You can't keep your job when your doctor says it would be detrimental for the child you are carrying and you can't keep your job when you are so far along your tummy doesn't fit between the sink and the wheelchair of the resident you are caring for! And who is the lazy one? Jackass! Yup, I called you a jackass. Why? Well, I will be making that pretty clear throughout these pages. Oh, and let me remind you that the skanks you chose to have affairs with were all

FATTER than me; idiot! Yup, I called your mistresses skanks… They all knew you were married and had children; stupid fuck! Need I also remind you that you were tipping the scale at a whopping 398 pounds before your gastric bypass surgery, so who is the fat ass, hmmm?

Okay, I am normally not that sharp tongued. Sarcastic, yes, but not sharp tongued. It is just that you can't write about what you have had to endure at the hands of your abuser and NOT let off a little steam. It isn't like, as the abused, you get the chance to stand up for your self and scream all the words you long to scream. We know all too well what the ramifications are for taking the risk of speaking our minds and attempting to stand up for ourselves don't we ladies?

I am sure you are wondering if I have any lasting scars from the emotional abuse I endured at the hands of my abuser. Why yes I do. If the words above I allowed to spill out over the pages did not indicate that then I guess I am not doing a good enough job of getting my point across. Back to scars though… It really isn't that big of a scar, but I know it will be with me, hiding out in the nether regions of my mind, for years to come. What scar? Oh, I can't rid myself of the lovely pet name of fat ass nor the phrase "worthless piece of shit". Even when I managed to get down to a size four I still believed I was a fat ass. I am no longer a size four and realize that it is not my weight that bothers me. All those names my abuser called me and all the nasty things he said made me uncomfortable in my own skin. How many of you ladies went on crash diets or crazy exercise plans or developed an eating disorder because you were told you were a fat ass? How many of you ladies turned into a control freak that felt a physical pain if they did not do everything perfectly? See, you are not alone! No, I didn't go on any crash diet or crazy exercise plan or develop an eating disorder, but I began to feel the overwhelming need to control my environment and do everything with a thirst for perfection. (I'm still battling with that doozy of a character flaw) No matter how hard you try you can never escape yourself. So, what do you do when you look in the mirror and only see the ugliness the man that supposedly loves you has repeatedly told you you are? I know those stupid affirmations experts tell you to say over and over again, while looking into the mirror, don't flipping work... Oh, I should say "don't work for me" or those same experts will try to rip me a new rear end. But come on! How do those experts honestly feel staring into the mirror and repeating "you're beautiful, you're loved, you're special, etc" is going to work? How is any of that supposed to erase years upon years of being told the complete opposite? It is 100% true that one negative, nasty, horrid comment from the person who "swears" they love you wipes away thousands of positive words we may have been told during our lives. I just read that back and I really sound like a bitter woman; I'm not. I have a habit of telling it like it is, even if it makes me look bad. I like to call it "letting it out and letting it go". How else are we supposed to heal if we don't vent?

I just realized something. I use a lot of quotation marks around certain words. I think I had better explain myself to any of those deciding to stick out this crazy ride of a book with me. I am sarcastic to a fault; there is no getting around it. Whenever you see quotation marks around a word or phrase; chances are I am doing the Doctor Evil finger marks when I say each word. So, picture me doing that when you come across those words or phrases... Oh, and the odds are I am probably wearing a smart ass look on my face too. Just a little FYI...

The second form up for discussion is Environmental Abuse. I bet a lot of you read that and asked, "What the hell is Environmental Abuse?" Well, in a nutshell I like to explain Environmental Abuse as a temper tantrum thrown by our abuser in the attempts to make us feel unsafe in our own home or surrounding environment. This generally involves, but is not limited to, the punching of walls or doors, the kicking of things, and pretty much throwing anything within reaching distance; hence the term "temper tantrum." I have learned though that our abusers would rather punch, kick, or break something they believe to be of importance to us versus something of theirs. You know, the if I can break this then I can break you mentality.

Damaging anything of mine was a problem for my abuser though. Since he felt everything under the roof of his castle belonged to him and only him, there was no way he was about to break any of his pretty pretty shiny things. I have tried for the past few days to write about how this form of abuse took shape for me and whether or not I have any lasting nasty after taste in my mouth. The problem was that I kept typing only to delete only to type only to delete only to type again. Anyone seeing a recurring theme in my madness to get all of my thoughts out? I didn't know what the deal was; writer's block maybe? Then the other day I was working out, going over my writing in my head, and realized what I was doing wrong. I thought I would be able to get through all the forms of abuse with out a hitch or at least without a huge one. I was totally wrong. When I sat down to continue with the forms of abuse all I could do was scream and cuss at the page. Don't forget though that I already apologized earlier for any of the madness I may type or language I may decide to use. As much as I feel it is important to get things off your chest, what I was writing was far from being productive and I knew it would neither help me or any woman reading my words.

Am I ready to begin telling you how Environmental Abuse effected me? No, I don't think I am. I think the reason I am not ready is because this form of abuse took a different twist for me. My right eye went completely blind in March of 1998 and my left eye finally lost all of its sight in September of 1999. The abuse only got worse once it dawned on that son of a bitch that I would never see it coming. All I want to do is yell and yell and yell at the bastard who thought he was such a big man for not only beating a woman, the mother of his children, the lady he supposedly loved, but a BLIND WOMAN. I flipping walked on eggshells day in and day out because of you!!! I was scared of my own fucking shadow because of you!!! Did it make you feel "all powerful" to sneak up on a blind woman and beat her, did it? God I wish I could beat you with a baseball bat until you feel every shove, punch, kick, choked throat, slap, throw to the ground, hair you ripped out of my head, and squeezed arm I felt for thirteen fucking years!! YOU DAMN BASTARD… YOU LOSER… YOU ARE NO MAN; YOU ARE A MONSTER, A BULLY, YOU SUCK!!!

See why I am not ready to tell you ladies how this form of abuse impacted my day to day life? I believe in God and the Lord through and through, but when I think of what I went through by the hands of my abuser I sometimes lose it. I am only human. What woman wouldn't want to confront the one who beat her on a daily basis and make him feel the same pain they did? The only problem with that ladies is our abuser will never ever ever feel the pain we went through. They will never shed the millions of tears we did. They will never live in fear like we did or still do. They have no compassion nor the ability to feel remorse nor the understanding of what it takes to actually love another human being. Hell, I highly doubt any person that abuses another can even love themselves… Crap, it took all that nasty writing for me to get to my point. I am not crying though and that is saying something.

WOW, maybe I shouldn't write while I am having my period. All those hormonal changes bring out that oh so lovely side that only my abusive first husband could bring out in me. Though if I had been able to spit out all of this emotional baggage over the course of those thirteen years then maybe I would not be doing it now; it is a thought. I am going to grab myself another cup of coffee (cinnamon flavored in case you are wondering) and will be back to jot more down on the page... Maybe this is a good time for anyone reading this to take a break too.

Alright, I just need to write about this and get it out of the way. First, imagine yourself blindfolded. I know darn well that any woman reading this, has been a victim of abuse, and felt any terror while being able to see will get a sense of what a nightmare it would be not to see your abuser coming at you. In a matter of seconds your mind reels with the thoughts of whether or not he is coming at you from behind or the side or head on; whether or not he has his hand clenched in a fist, or worse, like there actually being something held in that fist... How mad is he? Where can I run? Can I get to a place where he can't knock me around too much? What was that noise? Was it him, something outside the window, one of the kids? If I run to the left will he be able to catch me or maybe I should run to the right... God, please just let him get it over with quickly. Time seems to stand still when you are being abused... Why does it have to stand still? Please just stop lurking over me and get it done with. Being scared of what is coming is one of the abusers biggest weapons. You get hit so much that you already know what it is going to feel like. You have been pushed down, choked, kicked, and whatever else physically he feels compelled to do to you that you already know exactly how it feels when he is doing it to you and how it will feel when he is done. But you cannot escape the fear of wondering when he is coming after you.

Bad day at work; he'll take it out on you. House not clean enough; he'll take it out on you. Yard not pristine; he'll take it out on you. Kids "too loud"; he'll take it out on you. Mistress piss him off; he'll take it out on you. His "Mommy" say something to upset his fragile ego; he'll take it out on you. Now add to all of that the fact you have to walk around blind folded. You have no idea what is about to happen on a daily basis because you can't look your abuser in the eye and tell what is going on in his head. Then again, I don't think women who can see, and are a victim of domestic violence, can truthfully say they know what their abuser is thinking. On one hand the abuser's behavior is predictable and on the other hand it isn't. This is what adds to the fear of it all.

I think this form of abuse was the worst for me to have to endure. It took me years after being free of him to feel I could walk around my own home and not be afraid. You are supposed to feel safe in your own home... How can you do that when your assailant is your own spouse or boyfriend or hell even girlfriend? Please tell me how to feel safe. The nightmares follow you and so you try not to fall asleep. You find yourself putting your new furniture in certain ways so everything is up against a wall. See, if all the furniture is up against a wall then you know he can't come at you from behind.

What do you do when where you live becomes your prison; your living nightmare? How do you escape fear...How do you fight and rage against something you can't even see... I don't have the answers to any of those questions. Do I still live in fear, yes I do. It is not a high level of fear though and I pray it is not a false sense of security or I am really screwed for the rest of my life. I wish I could tell everyone reading this that there is a quick fix pill, but there isn't. The only true healer of all things is time. Know though that you are not the only woman to be afraid of a shadow, a door creaking, a car pulling into a driveway, or a footfall. I need a break from this if you don't mind. No, I am not crying; just need to walk around and shake off a couple of ghosts.

This would normally be the part where I sit back down in front of the computer and yell at the page as if it were my abuser. Sorry ladies, but I just don't have it in me this morning. I am full of sorrow today; not for me, but for the man that chose to beat me down for so long in hopes to make himself feel like a "real man". He'll always be a monster in my eyes and I pray our children do not turn out anything like him. I am also full of many questions like how could you hit me in front of our kids, how could you beat me while I was pregnant with each one of our children, how could you sleep so soundly knowing you caused another human being such physical and mental anguish… how, how, how, how? I know in my heart that these questions will never be truly answered, but they are still questions that will haunt me on my bad days.

I suppose many folks could possibly read what I write and ask, "How can you say all those nasty things about the father of your children" or "Aren't you afraid your children will read this and hate you for what you have said". Here is my take on that line of thought. I am writing the truth. I am writing how I feel. I am standing up for any woman who has been in my position and is too afraid to rage against the machine. If I am not honest with myself about what I went through, then how on earth can I expect my children to be honest or stay true to their beliefs or any of that? You can't break the cycle of abuse if you keep your mouth shut. You can't break the cycle of abuse if you aren't willing to step on some toes. And, if you think about it, I am only stepping on the toes of anyone who has raised their hand or voice beyond the point of no return.

I do want to share a bit of what I did in order to free myself from some of the fear I lived with day in and day out. When I was kicked out in 2005 I went to live with my big brother for about three months. I made sure my abuser did not have the address of where I was staying. Knowing my brother was only a bedroom away and between the door of the apartment and my bedroom helped. Once I moved into my own apartment, which was in the same complex as my brother, I made sure only family knew where I lived and they had to either call me before showing up or use a certain knock. I eventually took a huge step though and moved almost an hour away from my brother to a town I knew would have better resources for a blind woman.

I was a flipping mess at first and jumped at every little noise. That is when I turned to a local community center for women and asked for help. I began going to meetings for victims of domestic violence, I worked with the area police to arrange a password for my door in case I needed help, and I never ever ever opened the door if I did not expect anyone over or a delivery from the post office. Honestly though all of that only helped a little. I still wanted to pee my pants when I heard a knock at the door that I was not expecting, I still freaked out when I thought I heard his truck drive by, I still had the nightmares of him coming into my bedroom and beating me. I think the nightmares he left me with were one of the worst things for me. They were so darn real and I couldn't push him off of me and when I woke from the madness it still felt like his hands had been all over me. How many of you can relate to that? See, you're not alone…

I think the hard part about feeling completely secure in our new environment will always be difficult to accomplish fully. I hear many stories of women who planned for weeks upon weeks to escape their abuser. (It is hard enough to take a pee without your abuser knowing about it; imagine planning your escape from Hell). Anyways, I hear all these stories only to find out later that some of these women end up beaten, or worse killed, after their abuser spends a whopping $9.99 on line to find out just where their punching bag has run off to. How can we ever feel completely safe when we know a few bucks spent on a website can give our abuser all the information he needs to find us? It just sickens me…

I have been trying for the past few weeks to write about the next form of abuse on our list of Reality Checks; Social Abuse. My attempts have failed and led only to me repeatedly deleting what I typed. Part of it maybe because there is so much I want to say about this form of abuse and I don't want to leave anything out. Another part of it is probably because thinking about it sparks so many memories of what I went through. I want to go over what most of us endure before I spout off on what I went through specifically and the two ideas are clashing in a battle to get on the page first. I suppose all of this would be easier if I were some writer paid to sit and write about abuse in nice neat little chapters, show off pretty diagrams and pie charts, and give a list of statistics. But I am not a writer sitting here getting paid to write this nor someone who can put their abusive past into pretty diagrams, pie charts, and lists of statistics. I am a woman who has lived through Hell and feels it is important to spread the word that you are not alone in your fight to rid yourself of the stench of abuse that oozes from all of our pores each day that we allow ourselves to be victimized by another.

Social Abuse is somewhat of an odd title to attach to this form of abuse since the abuse itself revolves around isolationism. We can't actually be "social" when our abusers try so darn hard to keep us isolated. Social Abuse, like all other forms, can start subtly. All is fine in your world, or so you think, and the next thing you know your phone conversations are being monitored, outings with friends either end up with you having a tag along or become fewer and farther between, and family get-togethers simply fade into nothing. This is just the tip of the iceberg though because it is the goal of our abuser to keep us shut up in the prison they so lovingly call our "castle". I need to grab a cup of coffee and try to straighten out my thoughts before I type anymore. I don't want to repeat myself or leave anything out. I also don't want to risk losing anyone reading this due to my ramblings.

Alright, I am back with coffee in hand. Oh how I wish I had a Never ending cup of coffee that was always nice and hot and that alternated between flavors! Oh please, what coffee lover wouldn't want that? Anyways, back to the matter at hand… As I was saying, Social Abuse can start subtly. It doesn't stop at the monitored phone calls and watch dog behavior though. Those things snowball into not being able to volunteer at your children's schools, not being allowed to run errands alone OR at all, family get- togethers always revolve around his side of the family, and well basically not even being able to take a pee without our abuser knowing about it.

What is the point of this type of behavior? Well, I truly believe our abuser needs to keep us on such a tight leash in order to maintain his public image as the charming and loving husband or , as in my case, the unappreciated husband who tries so darn hard and still gets no love, support, or affection from his severely handicapped and demanding wife. It wouldn't be easy for our abuser to lie to the public, his friends, employees, or co- workers if we were seen out and about because then all those people our abuser has been lying to will begin to see the real truth. Let me clarify, if I may, that I will use the term "our abuser" from time to time throughout this book. Why, you ask? Well, if you take a moment to think about it, our abusers are all the same beast just in different skin…

Now, if our abuser cannot control the situation because we have a job with curious co-workers, caring friends who refuse to be ignored, or family that try to keep in touch with us then our abuser will do one or more of the following things:

-get a job where we work
-show up unannounced at our place of employment
-not allow us to work
-constantly call us when he cannot physically see us
-answer the phone for us
-not allow us to talk on the phone
-keep tabs on our cell phone, if we are lucky enough to have one
-eavesdrop on our phone calls
-not allow us to volunteer at our children's school
-not allow us to go to church or house of worship
-not allow us to make plans for parties, play dates, family holidays, and/or medical appointments if he cannot be there
-not allow you to have a set of car keys

Did any of that ring a bell for any of you ladies? I am basically telling you that your (our) abuser will go to any lengths to either keep an eye on you or screw with you so much mentally that you feel he is everywhere or make it so you are a prisoner in his home. Yes, I know I probably repeated myself in what I wrote above, but I am trying to make a point here. This type of behavior on the part of our abuser results in us being deprived of any sort of privacy or basic forms of freedom.

All the aforementioned is minor league stuff though; it gets worse. Our abuser becomes so obsessed with his public image that next thing we know we are not allowed to even work. He'll even go to the extent to have his friends drop in on us unannounced while he is away just in case we are "having an affair". See, our abuser will even lie to his friends about us in order to have help keeping us prisoner and isolated. If this sort of behavior fails then his only option is to constantly move us so we can't make friends, can't get a job for too long of a time; if at all, and we are moved farther and farther from our own family. So, no job means no nosy co-workers, no friends means no one to confide in, no family close by means no where to run. If it reaches this point your abuser has you exactly where he wants you and speaking from personal experience it is a shitty place to be.

I say it is a shitty place to be only because my lovely abuser took extra steps to keep me isolated from the outside world. As you know by now, I am blind. I was not allowed to have any screen reading software put on the computer for me to have access to email or the internet. Looky looky, he made it so I could not even communicate with distant friends or family via email; what a sweetheart. He also did not allow me to purchase a scanner with voice capabilities. This meant I could not read any mail that came into the house. I had no idea what bills were racking up, what mail was for me, nothing. Understand why it was so shitty? If you were to ask my abuser about all of this though he would more than likely have a good reason why I was not able to have the adaptive equipment I should have had as a blind person. It just really sucks that I was put through all of that for so long. I will never understand how my abuser woke up each day and didn't care that he was treating another human being with such cruelty. Ignoring the fact that I was now blind, denying me adaptive equipment (And no, a thirty minute demo that anyone can find on-line does not count as adaptive equipment), and figuratively keeping me in the dark about how he ran the financial side of the household was a horrible thing to do to me.

I have to take a side road for a moment... I just read back the above paragraph and became disgusted and nauseated over the amount of times I used the word "allowed". What the heck is that about? We ladies are adults, but somehow our lives became the property of our "loving significant other" and we now have a never-ending list of things we are not "allowed" to do or to have or to say or to think... Not allowed? Would an abuser, ANY ABUSER, please stand up and explain to those of us who have been victims of your rage how you can actually justify this list of what we are/are not allowed to do. Sorry to bring this point up to all of you abusers, but being in a so-called relationship with a woman does not mean you have the right to take away her freedom or sense of independence! At times I get incredibly angry when I think about how my first husband kept me locked away from my family, any folks that I could have been friends with, and from living life without fear of severe consequences. I am not saying he physically locked me away. I am saying that he had me so afraid to reach out to anyone that my daily conversations revolved around our children and what they did all day and what they watched on TV. I would have killed (figuratively) for an adult conversation! You get to a point that you honestly start praying a bill collector or telemarketer will call your place just so you can hear another adult's voice. I love my children, but years upon years of baby talk that only turned into little kid talk was depressing for me.

I took some time out to eat lunch and while I was sitting in my recliner, eating, a thought came to the forefront of my brain… Our abuser's enabling family! The thought both sickens me and saddens me… I bring this part up because if our abuser is "really good" then he will get his family in on the abuse too. His family members basically either live in a constant state of denial about the ugly behavior of their son/ stepson/ brother/ grandchild/ cousin/ nephew/ whatever or they fear his deranged behavior as much as we do and, in turn, help him keep us in line. What happens to a family member that won't go along with our abuser? Easy… that family member no longer exists to our abuser. He simply writes them off and bitches that "you are taking her side". It is pathetic, truly pathetic. My former abuser has this very type of a lovely family and I would love to say, "Fuck you" to all of them, but instead I'll just say that I hope you all rot in whatever private Hell you have created for yourselves for what you have done in order to keep my abuser from getting mad at you!!! You'd all rather sit back and listen to him whack me around or yell at me versus rocking the boat and forcing him to get some seriously needed help! I hope you all feel good about the fact you turned a blind eye to everything that was going on.

I suppose the abuser's enabling family should be lumped into the group of folks that would call this book of mine a work of fiction. I have learned the hard way that abusers and their families are incredibly dysfunctional and need help. I understand how an abuser, if cornered, will blame his behavior on how his parents treated him and then his parents will say they raised him that way because their parents treated them poorly and on and on and on. I am sorry, but stand up for what is morally right and break the cycle of abuse! There comes a point where the excuses need to stop and the healing needs to begin, but that can't happen simply by acting like the abuse is not going on. Just because abusers and their family members sweep all the horrible things done to us under the "Family Rug" doesn't mean that none of it happened!

So, what happened to me when it concerned this form of abuse? When my ex realized the bruises he left on me were coming into question he moved us and moved us and moved us and moved us and moved us. A total of fourteen times in a span of thirteen years. Now if you ask him why we moved so darn much he will blame me for it all; just thought I'd add that. Were any of you ladies moved place to place and then yelled at because all the moving around was all of your damn fault? I bet dollars to donuts that some of you know exactly what I am talking about. Anyways, when it came to the bruises, he got wise and made sure he didn't leave marks that were visible, but then what to do about the wife that was so mentally frazzled that she shook like a Chihuahua when ever she was in public or was asked how she was doing? He couldn't hide that, so he isolated me. By the end of my thirteen year prison sentence I was beaten down to the point that I had no hope of ever getting out. My life meant no real friends, no family, and no freedom and that was how it was going to stay…

I could expand more on what I went through when it came to Social Abuse, but it honestly is too painful for me to talk about without feeling compelled to scream vulgarities at the page or cry my eyes out or hit the nearest wall or drink myself into sweet oblivion. I will say this… I was verbally tormented to the point that I was ashamed of who I was. Who wants to be seen in public when they are constantly told they are a piece of shit or are embarrassing to be around because they are blind or that they aren't worth a dime? And who wants to try to have a relationship with their in-laws when they know their abuser has lied through his teeth about what his wife is like? He had me exactly where he wanted me… Too ashamed to show my face to anyone for too long and stuck inside taking care of his castle. I don't know what angers me more; the fact he took thirteen years of my life away or that I allowed it to happen.

I know what a lot of you are thinking right now after reading that last sentence; that I didn't "allow" any of it to happen. I did though… I did. Why didn't I stop the abuse? Why didn't I stand proud? Why didn't I do all that was necessary to get out of a horrible situation? I suppose it is easy to second guess yourself when you are free from the mental fuck show and physical pistol whippings. I don't like looking back at how weak I was; it hurts. Yes, I also look back to the less than handful of times I tried to stand up for myself. I remember what happened to me when I tried. I just don't want other women to go through what I did or feel they have no way out or that there is no future for a beaten down soul because there is. We may not see it while we are in the abusive relationship. We may not see it when we are trying so desperately to break free of the abusive relationship. Freedom will come though, life will return, love; real love; will sweep you off your feet if you allow it to. I promise…

This is also the part where a therapist, who has probably NEVER been in my position or yours for that matter, would cover my hand with theirs and make comments in a soothing tone of how none of it was my fault or I was in no position to stop my abuser or I did the best I could to survive a horrible situation. But did I really do enough? No, I didn't do enough, I didn't stand proud, I didn't fight back. Instead I did what I saw my mother do. I let it go in one ear and out the other (one of my mother's often used expressions) and put up with the crap because my children needed a father, I was never going to have anyone who could love me, and so on and so on. I don't blame my mother; I blame the cycle. I pray the cycle is now broken though and my children neither abuse another human being or are a victim of abuse when they come of the age where they feel they are ready to start a relationship with someone. Nothing personal, all you therapists and counselors and psycho-babblers, but I just second guessed myself in a previous paragraph, so what makes you feel any words from a professional will be utterly life changing? Change starts from within and, for me, with the Lord above; no insurance provider required…

The next form of abuse up for bids is Financial Abuse. Basically it is when our abuser controls all aspects of the money flowing into and out of the household. This form is what I like to call the "No win situation" form of abuse. With other forms of abuse there is a false glimmer of hope that if we just change what our abusers are yelling at us about then they can't yell at us anymore; at least not about that.

For example, he tells you that you are fat. Fine, you start running on a treadmill or doing exercises with the TV and limit what you eat. He says the house is a pig sty (which is probably not the case), so you just start cleaning three times during the day, if not more. My schedule was to clean as soon as he left the house, clean after the kids came back from school, and clean just before I thought he would walk through the door. Did it work? Hell no, but I had that false hope.

With Financial Abuse there is no chance for false hope that you can fix the situation. Our abuser complains we don't bring in a pay check and in the same breath screams that we will never work outside the home; what the hell? OK, so back to Financial Abuse. When I mean he has all the control of money matters I truly mean Has ALL CONTROL. First, he has total control of the bank account(s). If he is kind enough (hahahaha kind enough) to leave money with you it is probably only because a repair man is coming and you need to pay him. Your abuser isn't stupid enough to leave you a check because then you will have the account information and that is a no no. In my case my abuser didn't have to worry when he left out a check because I had no means of reading the account information off of the check; one of the downfalls of being blind I suppose.

Since he won't leave you with cash then he definitely isn't about to give you your own bank card. "Oh, but he took me with him to open the account. I am supposed to get a bank card." Yeah, you're "supposed to", but HE CONTROLS EVERYTHING and is not about to put that pretty bank card in your hot little hand. In my case, he gave me my bank card alright, but conveniently forgot to activate the card for me. You have dreams of having a credit card, so you can start building credit in your name; not going to happen. Our abuser won't hand over to you your own credit card, but I am here to say that doesn't mean he didn't apply for one in your name or put you on the card as an authorized user. See, it is not only the goal of our abuser to control the flow of money… It is also his goal to ruin your credit when he puts you both in debt.

Alright, if you are reading this and are still in that frame of mind where you think your abuser wouldn't "dare ruin his own credit just to ruin yours" then SNAP THE HECK OUT OF IT!!! Our abuser will ruin our credit along with his and then move around so much that the bill collectors can only find your butt and not his. If it happened to me then it can surely happen to any of you ladies. You are being abused on a daily basis; in some way, shape, or form; so what makes you think your credit report is sacred?

This form of abuse is also two fold. For one, if you have absolutely no access to money or funds then you can't run and leave him. For another, as I already mentioned, he will ruin your credit to a point where years after you finally get away from him you can't establish anything in your name without a co-signer. Financial Abuse, if you are lucky to escape your abuser, is like living with the mess of nuclear fallout. You think you are free from your abuser, because the big bomb dropped while you were residing with him, only to discover weeks or months or years later he got a loan in your name and gave the bill collector YOUR information before running away with his irresponsible tail between his legs. Or, maybe he racked up a huge credit card bill and since he put your unknowing behind on it as an authorized user it is your credit report that is jacked up. It is so much like living with a nasty after taste in your mouth that a toothbrush, economy size tube of toothpaste, mouth wash, and breath mints just can't get rid of. I became physically free from my abusive ex-husband just a tad over four years ago, but I have a current sports magazine sitting atop my hutch with his last name on it as a reminder of all the bills he racked up in my name. I am going to say the following out of pure sarcasm and truly don't mean it deep down, BUT you ladies that are not married yet might want to think about keeping your last name if you ever do tie the knot and hide anything with your social security number on it from your new beau.

You name it; he stuck my name on it. I honestly thought I had finally cleaned up the mess of his financial hold on me until I got a well known clothing store, located in just about every mall in America, calling me about a bill that was over $1000, another call from a collector for a bill close to $2000 (and they were about to sue him), and now this magazine subscription! Now can I safely say this specific magazine subscription is the result of my ex-husband doing something shady? Well, no I can't, but when my first name is spelled wrong, my former last name is correct, and that same name showed up on a totally different sports magazine that messed up my credit then it really doesn't take a rocket scientist to do the math. I did get some satisfaction out of all the mess with my credit though. Every time a bill collector called me asking for my ex-husband or his wife

(meaning me), I gladly explained we had been divorced for years and proceeded to give them every piece of personal information I could give them about him, his current line of credit(meaning significant other), his parents, and the name and contact information for his attorney.

I think I should add that not only did I have to put up with bill collectors calling my home looking for my first husband, they also called looking for his mother and her third husband. When it got to that point, my husband and I decided to get rid of our landline. Ridiculous isn't it? So ridiculous that even my parents and sister were called by bill collectors looking for my ex-husband and my brother received bills in the post with my first husband's name, but my brother's address. All the Financial Abuse you, and those in your family, go through is like stepping in dog shit that you never think you'll get off of your shoes! Not to mention if you have family members that are less than understanding of the

LILY ANNE BURNETT

situation and get on your case for what your ex or soon to be ex has done. After all that being said though, no more bill collectors calling my phone and I sleep very well at night, thank you very much…

Since your abuser needs to control you financially you may find that he doesn't allow you to check the mail or he leaves work to quickly drive by and check it before you can or he puts his billing address as some address other than your home address, which keeps it safely out of the reach of your prying eyes. If you can't see the bills then you can't see the mess of debt he is racking up in your name. Some abusers will even go to the morally depraved lengths to get a line of credit in one of your children's names. Oh please, pick your jaw up off the floor! See, he gets the line of credit in your children's name because they are minors and will never realize their poor credit is shot until they are older and try to get credit themselves. How do I know this? Somehow my daughter had a subscription to a music club before she was the age of ten; go figure… Isn't that sweet of him? Geez, if I had only known then what I know now, I would have saved all of that sort of crud. That way I could have taken pictures of all of it and added them to the book for "dramatic effect"! Don't think for one minute that I don't take time to read all this garbage back to myself and think, "She is making all of this up.", because I do. Those who have been abused and have had some of this stuff happen to them though know all too well that I couldn't make this stuff up out of thin air even if I tried…

Oh, so back to the "no win" situation. Ever hear this one? "You don't bring any money into this house or contribute to the bills and I am tired of your lazy ass!" But dear, you told me I wasn't allowed to work out of the house (of course you are only thinking this because actually saying it will bring a fist into your personal space), "You'll never fucking leave me because your sorry ass can't hold a job and without me you'll have no money and no way to support yourself. Oh, the kids? You won't be taking the kids from me either!", or my very favorite line, "your SSDI isn't worth shit and you may as not be getting anything!" What, I get disability? I have my own money? How come I never see any of it? Oh that's right… My disability check covers your truck payment and a new lawn of grass in your back yard or whatever else you spend my disability money on without my knowledge; jackass!

I was finally approved for disability in 2000 and I never got it away from him until October of 2004. That was out of pure luck in a way. In October of 2004 my lovely first husband abandoned me and our three children. Where did he go? I honestly have no idea. I am assuming it was to be with the employee that he was having an affair with at the time (oh look, another control trip for our abuser. Only this time he probably threatened to fire the poor gal if she didn't sleep with him; nice). Anyway, as soon as he left I called up Social Security and changed my personal information with them. This meant my check came to me and not into his bank account. Don't think the first call I got from him when he found out wasn't a doozie; man was he pissed. But dear, you told me my SSDI wasn't for shit, so why do you care that I took my money away from you? Him walking out gave me just enough freedom to take back my money and since he abandoned me and our three children how else was I going to provide for the four of us?

So, in a way I was sort of free, because I took back my SSDI, but I also really didn't have much money or a car or a support system. It took me a couple of weeks to think long and hard about "outing" my situation to our neighbors. I either had the choice to protect the public image of my abuser; my children's father; or to get off my ass and fight for myself and my kids. I chose the latter… This is when I left the house and slowly unloaded to my neighbors about what was going on. I began making Christmas wreaths and center pieces to sell at my children's school for extra money, I began selling beauty products, and I put two of our children on the free lunch program at school which helped a lot.

Okay, so I have some money in my pocket, I am confiding in our neighbors, I am growing a spine… didn't last long. A few months later my then-husband wanted back home and gave a slue of excuses and bullshit lies, so dumb ass me opens the door wide and helps him move his crud back in. But, don't forget my state of mind at the time… I had three children constantly asking why their father didn't want to be with them and would rather be with his girlfriend (yup, he flaunted his mistress in front of our children), I felt I was still that worthless piece of shit I was so lovingly called, and I honestly still felt everything was my fault and if I could just manage to be perfect then all would be alright for my family. Oh, he came back alright and soon wanted my SSDI money back in his account. Somehow I surprisingly stood my ground and said "No, because I need the money for our children and you could walk out again". That went over like a lead balloon and all Hell broke loose. I was right though because he left again, only to come back, only to leave again. Oh, don't feel sad about that fact because my spine started growing even stronger.

My abuser was all the way in Florida at the very end and I was left happily, if you can use that term, in Texas. I was doing the freedom dance every chance I got. Don't think him being in Florida meant the abuse stopped because it didn't. Even though I received constant nasty phone calls about how worthless I was, how I was having an affair, how he needed my SSDI, and so on and so on and so on I managed to get stronger. I don't think he realized miles between us would diminish the hold he had on me, but when you have children you have to raise and be strong for then you do what you have to do. Not to mention my friends stepped up and gave me constant support and words of encouragement. The kids had more freedom too and got a break from listening to their father yell and scream and stomp around the house. I got them out to neighborhood barbecues and parties and the house was finally quiet and becoming an actual home; no more walking on eggshells for any of us.

Man, those were some wonderful times I had with my children once their father was in Florida. I still reminisce from time to time with the kids about those days. I know my children miss Texas; I miss Texas too, but I can't turn back the hands of time for them or for me. I hope to have the chance to make more memories like that with my children. Memories full of happiness and love. Memories they will be able to tell their own children about someday.

Unfortunately, that only lasted a few short months. He was in Florida, I was left back in Texas to sell the house (because I swear hun, I'll make this marriage work), and I had to move in with his oh so wonderful state of denial/enabling parents. Why did he lie and say he would try harder to make the marriage work? Well simple, I was bringing in money with my SSDI, I was bringing in money with the Christmas decor and selling beauty products, and I was fighting to get a settlement from a car accident I was in and he wanted all of that money in his bank account. So, why all the way to Florida? For starters, his new mistress lived there and second; which is his pathetic reason; "We need to get as far away from Texas as we can if we are going to start a new life. We need to get away from all of the negative people and rumors and stuff…" No, I am not joking. He actually sat in our family room and gave me that line of bull and I stupidly sat there and believed it. He only wanted to get as far away from Texas as possible because he was screwing his employee and everyone around our neighborhood knew exactly what a pig he was!

So, stupidly by the end of July of 2005 I flew with two of the kids to Florida to be with the loving reborn husband and our oldest child he had flown out to Florida in order to keep a hold on me. God, I was so damn stupid; well, partly. No sooner did we get settled into an apartment when he wanted my SSDI and wanted to know when my settlement was going to come. I found a friend in a lady who lived a building over and unloaded everything to her. She helped me get my own bank account so I could keep my SSDI checks to myself and a place to deposit my settlement check. Am I really becoming financially free of the bastard? I thought so until the settlement check came and my friend told me they left my first husband's name on it along with mine. I called the attorney right away and asked for a new check in only my name and told him why. I mailed back the bad check and had to wait, for what seemed forever, for the new check. I got the check, deposited it, and was kicked out of the apartment a couple of weeks later so his current roll in the hay could move in. Do I think if I gave him my settlement check that our marriage would have been "saved", no I am not that stupid...

Being kicked out didn't mean I was safe guarded from Financial Abuse though. I found an IRS bill for $1800 two days before I was kicked out and was told if I didn't pay it then I would never see the kids again once I was gone, so I paid it. Once I was outta there it turned into "pay my credit card bills off or you won't see the kids for Christmas!", or "Pay the loan off because your name is on it too and I'll keep the kids from seeing you come the next school break." Or the constant yelling calls from him basically all saying, "You better fucking pay my bills off or I'll make your life a fucking Hell and you will never see the kids again! Pay my fucking bills you bitch!". There is no contest between me keeping my money and becoming financially sound and giving up money in order to see the kids. Granted I needed the money, but

I needed my kids more. That is just one of the massive differences between myself and the father of my children. I chose the children over any amount of money and he tries to control the children, so he can have money (tax deductions, no child support to pay, etc). It is all about money for him; money, money, money!

I bet you are all wondering how much he squeezed out of me before the Gravy Train stopped. Give me a second and I will add it up. Yeah, I maybe a tad sick in the head for being able to remember all the money he extorted from me, and maybe you might feel I need therapy, but this is what years of abuse does to you; gives you a mind like a steal trap. Can I get a drum roll please… $10,896 and some change. Once the divorce process started though he couldn't threaten me anymore because I just didn't care. I was learning that pain is not permanent, words are just words, and his twisted abusive hold on me was dwindling. He was beginning to realize that too and wasn't liking it. I have since wiped all of his mess off of my credit report and receive no more calls from bill collectors. I did put three of the debts he racked up in my name in the divorce decree for him to pay in full. You guessed it; he ran from those for as long as he could. I actually had to send a copy of the part of the divorce decree that stated my ex-husband was legally responsible for one of the bill so they would stop hounding me. Last I knew he also still owed a popular cell phone company a whopping $1200 and some change. All I know is I got that off my credit report also, so who cares if he pays it or not. He has a new wife now with great credit that he can start ruining; hahahahaha.

I should have kept a record of the day the Financial Abuse all stopped so I could celebrate each year with a Free from Financial Abuse Anniversary. Yes, this form of abuse is long lasting once you are free of the beast causing all of the trouble, but it is also the form of abuse that does not leave a lasting mark on your soul. Can I get an Amen!

What are we on, like the fifth form of abuse? I believe it is and that form is Religious Abuse. Yup, even religion; I keep telling you ladies that nothing is sacred to our abuser when it comes to controlling us in any way possible! Religious Abuse can be incredibly effective if your religion or spirituality is of importance to you. On a side note though, if your religion or spirituality is strong within you then your abuser can't take that away completely. I did have a few lines typed up about this form of abuse and just deleted them. I wrote them out of pure anger and what good is that really. Not to mention the fact I started this project so long ago and what I felt back then when I wrote about this form of abuse is not how I feel today.

When I was kicked out and forced to leave my children, I felt utterly alone. I cried to God, for what seemed like days on end, asking Him why He was doing this to me; putting me through Hell and allowing my abuser to have all the control. Then I slowly began to realize that God was not responsible for what I was going through, but would be the reason I got out of it. Once this fact sank into my mind and soul; my writing took on a new look and I went from being the raving lunatic to a more productive writer.

If you have made it this far with me and have listened to what I am saying, then we can all come to the ultimate conclusion that each form of abuse is a fight for control over us by the abuser and not because some Higher Power has a twisted sense of humor. Here is the kicker though, and it didn't occur to me when I started this little journey of mine on paper, our abuser can take everything away from us, but not our soul. Nice to know that little secret isn't it? He can beat us down verbally, he can isolate us to the point he thinks we are "alone", and even cause us such physical pain that we'd like to curl up in a ball and die, but he CAN NEVER TAKE OUR SPIRIT! Oh, he may crush it, but he can't control it. As I said in the beginning of this book, "you are not alone" and it didn't matter your age, race, cultural background, or religious preference… I am not here to pressure you into believing in God or tell you that you must believe in Jesus Christ. What I am saying though, whether you believe or not, is that a Higher Power is watching over you and keeping the one part of you that can't be touched very safe.

I will step off my soapbox for a moment and explain why your abuser doesn't like religion. Religion means going to church or other place of worship, going to that place of worship means getting to know other people, getting to know other people creates a risk that the abuser will be discovered, and then the control over you is lost; he can't have that. Unfortunately, if you have a strong faith in a religion and want your children to experience and be a part of your faith; it's not going to happen. Well, at least it won't happen the traditional way of church on Sundays and Wednesdays; depending on your faith.

When children are involved the Religious Abuse will extend to them unfortunately. One way or another (unless your abuser is dead or in jail) your children's father will keep them from attending church, or Vacation Bible Study, or anything that involves allowing the children to meet a group of people who sincerely care about their welfare. If your abuser didn't want you pouring your heart out to other people he sure as heck isn't about to let his children spill the beans about his abusive ways. Control, control, control; sad…

Also if there are children involved and if, sadly, they live full time with your abuser (don't be shocked. I know of many instances where the battered mother is screwed out of having her children with her. Nothing is permanent though) this means your abuser still holds the "Religious Abuse" card. You want your children to grow spiritually, but no matter what you say to your abuser he WILL NEVER LISTEN TO YOU AND YOUR

CHILDREN WILL NOT BE ALLOWED TO ATTEND ANY KIND OF WORSHIP SERVICE!!!

Yes, I shouted that last line. That is only because I begged my children's father to let them attend Sunday school and all he did was lie through his teeth and say he would. Oh, but that means he would actually have to take time out of his incredibly busy life to give the children what they wanted and craved; can't have that. This brings us to the previous statement that faith cannot be taught to our children in a "traditional" manner. Fine, you won't bring the children to God… I'll make darn sure I constantly bring God to them every single moment I see the children or talk to the children. God blessed me with those three gorgeous children and saw me through all of the abuse, so there is no way I am not going to teach the children about faith in a Higher Power.

Again, if you truly have a strong faith then this form of abuse won't do much damage. Oh, your abuser can spit nasty comments at you about your faith, keep you from a place of worship, keep your children on a tight leash too, but it means absolutely nothing. What ever Higher Power you believe in, if you are fortunate enough to, will always be there in the brightest of days and the darkest of times. For me, God was a presence that my abuser could never have control over and could never charm. God was and is the one being in my life that my abuser could not keep me from. Sanctuary is in me; not a church or other house of worship. I am always thankful for my faith… the spirit I could not be robbed of. Of course this little tidbit of information does upset our abuser. He can mock our faith all he wants, but in the end he is seen for what he is, a bully. Some abusers will even go to the extent to sound pathetically stupid by saying, "you're cheating on me with God!". My only advice to you ladies is that if you have faith don't let it go and if you are lacking faith then you may want to try to find some. The power of prayer is both healing and strengthening; use it…

SURVIVING DOMESTIC VIOLENCE

The next form of abuse is Physical Abuse. This is a rough topic to talk about as well as read about. So, if you ladies don't mind I am going to stray off the path a little bit in order to purge my heart and mind of all the nasty things I would have liked to have said to my abuser. I say "liked to have said" because I no longer wish to confront him with my words. As we have discussed earlier our abusers want one thing, control. They don't want to listen to us ramble about what they did to us because in their eyes they have done absolutely nothing wrong. Long story short; confronting your abuser in the hopes he will sincerely apologize for all the damage he has done to you is fruitless and will never happen. If your abuser doesn't even care about himself down deep how on this Green Earth do you think you can get him to care about what he did or is still doing to you? Okay ladies... here I go! I hate you... I hate you for every nasty word you spat at me... I hate you for every slap to the face... I hate you for throwing me to the ground and kicking me repeatedly in the stomach... I hate you for each handful of hair you ripped out of my head... I hate you for every time you slammed me into a wall... I hate you for constantly moving us and constantly saying it was my fault we had to move... I hate you for calling me a whore... I hate the mere fact you breathe... I hate how you spread your need for control to include our children... I hate you for forcing me to lie to my family... I hate you for every time you pushed me to the floor... I hate every time you threw me into the closet and beat me while I had no where to run... I hate you for choking me until I couldn't breathe... I hate you for picking me up by my throat only to tossed me back down... I hate you for each car ride that ended up with you punching my head into the window... I hate you for every time our children had to watch your rage... I hate you for beating me while I was pregnant... I hate you for calling me fat... I hate you for telling me I was a worthless piece of shit... I hate you for calling me stupid... I hate you for taking a body that didn't belong to you; married or not... I hate you for every lie you told to me... I hate you for spitting in my face... I hate every squeezed and bruised right arm... I hate you, I hate you, I hate you... I hate you for every time you choked me with my own necklace... I hate you for thinking jewelry would shut me up... I hate you for all the lies you told to make yourself look good and me look like the horrible wife... I hate you for the betrayal... I hate you for every tear I shed... I hate you for making me doubt my own self-worth... I hate you for all the head games... I hate you for making me afraid in my own skin... I hate you for making me walk over two miles round trip after neck surgery and with Three children just so I could drag back groceries... I hate you for making me walk through the San Antonio airport without a guide or my cane because you were angry with me... I hate you for making me feel worthless because I was blind... I hate you for yelling at me and hitting me over a football game... I hate you for trying to break my neck... I hate you for forcing me out of the apartment and making me leave our children with you... I hate you for flaunting your affair with your employee in front of our children... I hate you for blaming me for everything that went "wrong" in your life... I hate you for thinking you will never reap what you have sewn... I hate you for turning me into a basket case... I hate you for the mere fact that you exist... I hate you for your inability to care about nothing and no one; save for money... I hate you, I hate you, I hate you... I hate the fact you weren't man enough to end our marriage the right way before starting your multiple affairs... I hate the fact you will never change in my eyes... I hate you for pushing me down stairs... I hate you for putting our children last and you and your mistresses first... I hate the fact that you are so cruel... I hate the fact I allowed you to turn me into someone who needs to type this above list of things she hates about another person...

As I was typing this nasty list yesterday I heard the chime letting me know I had email. Just so you know, while typing the I Hate List I never shed a single tear. It was as simple for me to type the above list as it is for me to type out a grocery list or recipe; nothing more. Anyways, I heard the email chime and went to see who had emailed me. It was my favorite gal in the world, Jules! Of course I immediately stopped writing my list of hates and went straight to opening her email. It was simply entitled "Friendship". I cried and laughed at the same time. I was crying both out of sadness because I miss Julie and because the email was so damn funny.

I need to explain a bit about Jules to you ladies, I think, in order to make you all understand what an impact this very woman has on my life, heart, and soul. She'll probably even threaten to kill me once she finds out I have added this side road to my book; who cares, she knows I love her! I met Julie and her family when they moved across the street and three houses down from me in San Antonio. Well, I met her husband first, but that is another story for another day. I met her and instantly every fiber in my being wanted to hug her and dump everything that was wrong in my life into her lap. Did I do this, of course not. That would have scared the woman away! I only saw her every once in awhile at first and so we didn't click right away. Soon though the weather was nice and everyone on the street was out in their drives cooking on the grill or sitting in lawn chairs. Our kids started playing together and my then-husband tried to portray us as a loving couple.(Remember he needs to maintain the perfect public image) God, how I wanted a moment alone where I felt free to unload to this woman I saw as a rock of unwavering strength! That day never happened until November of 2004; almost two years after meeting her.

I better add here that Jules is at present a Major in the Air Force and exemplifies a lot of the qualities I felt I had until my then-husband beat them out of me. Oh, I am not saying Jules is perfect, wears a halo, and carries a harp. It is just that she was where I thought as a girl I was going to be when in my thirties. Okay, not the Air Force part, but a mom; a career woman; a contribution to society; someone using the brains and talent God gave her...

As I wrote earlier it took me a couple of weeks to decide if I was going to "out" my situation to the neighbors or keep up the façade my husband had built around our "loving home". Julie is who I opened up to and I will never forget that day because it started me on a road of freedom that I was not willing to stray from without a fight. Jules came knocking on my door one early morning all dressed up in her camouflage and ready for work. Now how on God's Green Earth could anyone possibly see this display of strength, honesty, and honor and not unload? I know what most of you are probably wondering; how can a blind woman see all of what she just described. Answer? Jules radiates all of the qualities I just mentioned and I knew what she wore to work, duh...

My husband had been out of the house and living who knows where, I was a tempest of emotions, I was struggling with keeping my children on an even keel, and I had wanted that very morning to happen for so damn long. I wanted someone I could truly and finally call a friend and here she was standing on my front porch. When it comes to Julie I have never looked back and I love her for all the gifts even she doesn't realize she has given me... Okay, now I am crying... shit... I have no Kleenex near my computer; hold on... I got the Kleenex and managed to stop the flow of tears until I had to go back and make sure what I wrote actually made sense and look what happened; I am crying again! I will stop here because I know I will talk about the importance of women friends later on and I really have to get back on the subject of the forms of abuse.

So, now we are officially on the form of abuse known as Physical Abuse. This form may sound clear cut by its title, but it is not. It includes Any unwanted physical contact and is usually repetitive. This means it just doesn't include the obvious slap, push, kick, or whatever else our abuser chooses to do to us on a large scale to hurt us. It also includes him getting into your personal space to the point you may trip and fall over something or knock into something. It also includes being injured by anything our abuser decides to pick up and throw at us. He doesn't need to physically touch us himself in order to physically abuse us; remember that. I also believe, in some twisted way, our abuser feels he "really isn't doing anything wrong" if he can chalk it up to us being clumsy or because he didn't physically touch us.

I skipped ahead for a moment to read over what I typed, which seems ages ago, and I am in such a different frame of mind today that I am going to delete what I typed. As you should all know by now, I don't really like to type out of anger. What I read, and subsequently deleted, was written out of anger; can't have that. Instead I read over what I typed, deleted it, thought about it, re-worded it, and now it makes more sense to me. I didn't type it out of anger this time. I typed it while in the "Cowering Dog" phase of my recovery. You are going to ask me what the "Cowering Dog" phase is, aren't you...

How do I put this... Alright, imagine a dog that is beaten repeatedly by its master only to come back with its tail between its legs, shaking, and with a look of "I know it is all my fault, good Master" in its deep brown eyes. Well, that dog is us and I mean ALL OF US. We are beaten down to the point that we are nothing more than a mutt to our abuser and he has become the Master. Man, how pathetic that whole situation is; from the blushing bride to the cowering mutt in the corner. And what is more pathetic is we still end up that cowering dog for months, even years, after we thankfully escape the abuse. We still think we are truly that mutt he told us we were, we still feel all of the mess was our fault, and we still believe if we crawl back with our tails between our legs then all will be happy happy joy joy with the fairy tale ending happily ever after; whatever…

Well, when I wrote the crud about Physical Abuse earlier I was already living in my own place, but still held the belief that everything that happened to me was because I "didn't behave" and that if I was a good mutt that all the madness would leave my abuser. I was hundreds of miles away from him, but one simple phone call had me back in the corner cowering with my tail between my legs and a glass of bourbon and Sprite in my hand to drowned my fear, shame, and guilt that the last thirteen years had been all of my fault. Wow, I have come a long way since then…

I should get back to the obvious when it comes to Physical Abuse and stop talking about myself. In many cases it starts subtly; like all other forms of abuse; and is generally something like a slap followed by the infamous words of "Oh baby, I'm so sorry" or "Oh babe, it'll never happen again, I promise" or "Look what you've gone and done!" or "You made me do it!". That last one was my personal favorite and apparently my abuser's as well since he used a few variations of it on me over the years. Here is a thought… Did I hold a gun to your head and force you to punch me, slap me, kick me, push me, choke me, and anything else you felt compelled to do? No, I didn't think so. Nothing irks me more than a man that beats on his woman and then has the audacity to blame it all on her. Take some flipping responsibility for your anger!

Physical Abuse, like other forms of abuse, does not just effect us. If there are children in the picture all these forms of abuse I have talked about will also have a negative effect on them. Our abuser, when in a fit of rage, seems to either forget the children are in the room or within ear shot of what is going on. I will use my childhood as a prime example of the effect it has. My father would drag me into our kitchen, sit me down on the floor by the sink, and tell me the following, "Now, you had better listen to all of this and pay attention because this is what a real marriage is all about!" and then he would begin to verbally and physically abuse my mother. Great Dad, thanks! You taught me that was what marriage was all about and I went and married a man that would prove your point until he nearly killed me!

Speaking from experience, I know what it is like to be a child raised in an abusive home. You live in that same state of fear; when is the shit going to hit the fan… In hind sight I realize even as a child I felt utterly alone, that no other child was going through what I was, and that I would have to put up with it until I came of age and got the heck out of the house. Yes, I realize I had an older brother and sister, but I never confided in them. It was like we all had our own little battle to fight and none of us were winning. Geez, I went from an abusive childhood to an abusive marriage; talk about being screwed from birth! But, that is a prime example of the "cycle" and its effects on a child. The child hears it, day in and day out, growing up and assumes that is just how life/love/relationships with others work. You are either the predator or the prey. Neither one of these choices are a good thing, but if the cycle is not broken then these are the only choices one has.

Physical Abuse is also typically committed along with other forms of abuse; there is no getting around it. You can be a victim of other forms of abuse and at first never be touched physically, but it will always escalate unless you get the heck out of Dodge. Sorry ladies, but that is the truth. If you think you are safe because he only calls you a name here or slams a door there or something else non-physical to you, you're not. Eventually what ever it is that has put the rage in the man you are involved with will not be appeased by a mere name calling or door slamming. The rage will over take him and he will beat you and beat you and beat you. There is no cure for him and the only hope for you is escape.

Some of you may feel I am sounding melodramatic, but I have lived it all for thirteen years and am telling you like it is. I have no other option, but to tell you ladies like it is. I need for you to understand completely that you are not alone anymore. No matter what your abuser says or does to you, you are not the only one experiencing it and there is hope. I swear there is hope, no… I promise there is hope. If you have managed to stay with me up to this point then either you know I am right in what I say or you are beginning to pray that I am. Baby steps… that is all I am asking for. Life is scary, abuse is scary, running towards the door or window of freedom is scary; I know that all too well.

I bet you are all wondering if I have any lasting emotional scars from this lovely form of abuse. Why yes, I do. I am a wound up ball of madness that I know in my heart will go off on anyone stupid enough to try to touch me physically in a negative way. I have so much rage bottled up inside for every time my first husband smacked me around or pushed me around or anything else he chose to do to me. This is a rage that, unfortunately, can't be stamped out of me by exercise or therapy or a Happy Pill. All I can say is I feel sorry for any man who tries to hurt me physically because they will have thirteen years of pent up rage unleashed upon them.

I need to stop for now because I took a moment to start a load of laundry and hence lost my train of thought. I'll get right back into the groove of things tomorrow morning though with cup of coffee in hand. I am back just like I said I would be; even got the coffee. Though I only spend a couple of hours writing each morning I walk away from the computer and spend my day with restless thoughts of what I finished writing. I don't do this to torture myself, but more as a way to know where I want to begin writing the next day. This morning I want to continue with the concept that we, as the abused, are like cowering dogs. I think this is important to bring up again because we are discussing Physical Abuse.

As I wrote yesterday, we are like the cowering dog in the respect that we keep going back to our abuser in the hopes he will love us and we can be the good mutt he demands that we be. But, we are also like that cowering dog because there is something about the form of Physical Abuse that makes us eventually desensitized to all of it. Do you understand what I am trying to say? It is like I said earlier… We get to the point that we know what the punch is going to feel like, how long it will hurt, and how eventually the pain fades away. I think knowing that physical pain from abuse does not, in most cases, last forever we just muster through it and then forget about it. Think about it ladies… It is not so much the Physical Abuse that scares us as it is the fear of it coming. Just like the cowering dog; it isn't afraid anymore of the beatings because it knows it is inevitable, but it does cringe every time its Master's hand moves or voice is raised. Any of this sounding familiar? Knowing we are in a constant state of fear is a complete high for our abuser. I'll even go out on a limb to say that it wouldn't surprise me if our abuser gets just a tad aroused sexually from all the control he feels he has. That is a sick realization to come to, but it is the truth. I'll be right back. No, I am not out of coffee. I have to get my winter cap and toss it on my head. I'll explain…

I am back. Why the winter cap, you ask? Well, as I said a few sentences ago that physical pain, for the most part, fades. Unfortunately, I have a physical pain that will never go away courtesy of my abuser. I have neuralgia on the left side of my head. What is neuralgia; a fancy term for nerve pain that can be caused by trauma. In my case, this pain means sleepless nights/days, loss of equilibrium, nausea, high sensitivity to touch over the entire left side of my head, sensitivity to light, and hair loss. I could go on, but what would the point be; you get the picture.

In the early Spring of 1994 my then-husband felt the need to repeatedly punch the left side of my head while he was driving down the road. I guess maybe he thought he would make his point more clearly if he punched my head, with every shouted word, into the passenger side window; who knows. Shortly after this pattern of behavior started he moved us to Florida and then Texas. I never noticed the pain until I moved back into colder weather. So, now once the temperatures start hitting the forty degree mark and lower I have to either wear a winter hat, use a heating pad, or tough it out. There is no cure for the excruciating pain and there is, unfortunately, no pill to alleviate the symptoms. Hmmm, where to go from here... Let me go over what I wrote. Maybe I have gotten all my thoughts about Physical Abuse down on so-called paper.

For the most part I have covered all that I feel necessary when it comes to Physical Abuse. Something is nagging at me though and I can't quite figure out what it is. It is like I am missing something, but what the heck is it? ESCALATION! I want to warn you more about the escalation of the physical violence that either is or will be put upon you by your abuser. As I stated before, the other forms of "head game abuse" won't be enough for your abuser over time and I highly suggest you listen closely to the words shouted at you by your abuser. In those fits of rage your abuser may drop clues as to what he will, down the line, do to you. It is like he is testing the waters first to see what you will put up with and what will appease his anger. I am sorry if this is turning your stomach and making you want to vomit. How do you think typing about all of this makes me feel? I realize something new about my once abuser each time I sit down in front of this computer and it sickens me.

I am going to use myself again as an example. When I met my first husband in college he was most definitely testing the waters with me. How much could he yell at me, how much could he push me around, how much could he threaten me without me walking away… For about the first year his favoritely used threat was, "I'm going to snap your fucking neck!". That threat turned into him choking me. The choking turned into picking me up by my throat and either slamming me into a wall or throwing me down to the ground or tossing me on to the couch. In the end all of that turned into the horrible realization that he was going to break my neck and either paralyze me or kill me in front of our three children. The day he kicked me out of the apartment he was in a fit of rage, all three children were in the apartment, and I was wearing a hard C-collar from recent neck surgery. Before stomping his way out of the apartment he screamed every nasty name he could think of at me, he shoved me around the apartment into anything he could, and knowing my neck was vulnerable he told me he would break my neck if I did not leave. What choice did I have? I had already been on the receiving end of his choke hold and I knew if he got my C-collar off and his hand around my neck that it was going to be over. As a mother I hated having to leave, but I also knew my children would not have a mother today if I didn't. I am no good to my children if I am paralyzed or dead… Paralyzed or dead… Even for a beaten down mutt they, I am sure, would choose to run. It hurt to leave my kids that Friday morning, most definitely, but I am here today and am able to hug my kids, hike with my kids, and wrestle with my kids. What would you have done in my shoes?

Our oldest son remembers things more clearly than the other two, but his father even has that covered. How, you ask? "Well, all of that was in the past." It is easy for the one doing the abusing to say "that is all in the past" because they feel nothing they did

was wrong; that it was all in our heads; that it was no big deal…
No big deal indeed. I think what upsets me the most about the
physical abuse is that my ex-husband tries to minimize the Hell he
put the mother of his children through. Sadly, our abusers will
never fess up to being the monsters they really are. I truly think
my ex-husband believed the shit he shoveled when saying, "You
made me hit you, you made me do this, this is all your fault, and
so on and so on and so on…". It is not my life long dream to
continually remind the beast of what he did to me during our
marriage. It is my life long pursuit to make sure it never happens
to our children though. If that means I talk with all of our children
when they ask me questions then that is what I will do. I refuse to
sit by quietly anymore about domestic violence. My first husband
punished me for years because of who knows what and I neither
want that same nightmare to happen to another woman or my
three kids. I am sorry, but you can't make our children forget what
you did to their mother by saying, "That was all in the past".

Bear with me ladies for we are almost done going over the
various forms of abuse. I believe we only have two left to cover.
Though it wouldn't surprise me that when I am finally done
writing this book, organizations worldwide will have come up
with more forms of abuse or have given the forms I have covered
different names. I need coffee (no surprise there) and I will get
back to typing…

I am about to go off on a rant again ladies, so hold on to your
seats… Know what two phrases I pretty much hate hearing?
Well, I used to hate hearing them and refuse to use them unless I
honestly mean them. I have a hard time with the phrase "I'm
sorry" and "I love you". I'm sure you are all probably thinking
that would mean I don't want to hear "I love you" from my own
husband; not true. I have gone from hating the phrases to
doubting those who just toss those same phrases around. Am I

making any of this clear? Let's try this... My first husband used to beat me and then have the nerve to say, "I'm sorry" or put the two phrases together to say, "I'm sorry and really do love you". Here is a clue for all you abusers out there who think you can beat the tar out of your woman and then stupidly think "I'm sorry" will be the cure-all for the pain you have inflicted upon her... Saying, "I'm sorry" or "I love you" means absolutely nothing when you keep repeating the fucked up behavior day in and day out. Would you abusers honestly think we loved you and were sorry if we beat you or screamed at you or pushed you down a flight of stairs or ripped handfuls of hair out of your head? Could we just bat our pretty eyelashes and say, "Oh baby, I am so sorry and I truly love you; truly I do"? I highly doubt it. So, why on Earth do you think we believe you when you say you are sorry or that you love us? (Cleansing breath) And that is why I really don't care for those two phrases. Show me that you are sorry; show me that you love me. Last I checked, abusing another person was not the universally accepted way to show you care.

I am not really thrilled about any forms of abuse, but this one turns my stomach ten fold and makes me want to run for a toothbrush and Brillo pad. Oh, and throw in some severely hot water and industrial strength soap. Any of you ladies want to guess at the name of this form of abuse? I'll give you three guesses and I am sure you won't need the last two. It is Sexual Abuse, but honestly let's just call it what it is for crying out loud; it is rape.

Before I go off on this little subject I will give the informal definition of it. Sexual Abuse: participating in any sexual act, against your inner will, to make your significant other happy or appease his rage. How is that NOT considered rape? It is hard enough to come forward to the public and admit your significant other has abused you physically or mentally or whatever. How are you supposed to speak out about "Sexual Abuse" when we, as the abused, are already stigmatized by the public for crying wolf or over dramatizing our situation? I have seen enough of the public's perception of rape to know that if we say ANYTHING about what is being done to us sexually that it won't be considered rape. What, just because you are in some form of a relationship with someone then that automatically means we "like" what is being done to our bodies sexually? Some where down the line of our society's development it decided that if you are dating someone then it is not rape, if you are engaged to someone then it is not rape, if you are married to someone then it is not rape, if you are a man and a woman takes advantage then it is not rape, or better yet, "she was asking for it because the way she was dressed".

As you can probably tell I feel very passionate about this subject and I am not sure if I can say enough about it. It is hard enough to come forward an admit you are being sexually abused, but then how do you prove it? This is another one of those no win situations, but this time it is one with the public and not your abuser. All I know is that, as the abused, you do what ever it takes to just survive the situation you are in. To endure it for any length of time and then "out" yourself is traumatic at best. You manage to get free of the madness only to be told by the public that you are full of shit. This is why those of us being abused on a daily basis say nothing at all. We live through a nightmare only to be told we are over exaggerating. And what pisses me off even more is that those folks pointing a finger and saying we are over exaggerating are the same folks who have never been in our position! It is so damn easy for outsiders to say, "Why didn't you leave. Why didn't you call the police? Why, why, why?". To those of you who ask such stupid questions… Why don't you join the Battered Ladies Club for awhile and stop putting those of us, who have lived through Hell, through yet another flipping Hell!! I have to deal with the laundry, but I promise this time I WILL NOT lose my train of thought…

I am back, but doing the laundry sparked a memory that I need to rid my brain of before I can get back to what I was talking about. My current husband, who I know loves me dearly, thinks I am a little control freak when it comes to putting the laundry away. He is all too right and I will explain. When I was married to my first husband I learned right away that ALL of his clothes were to be hung so they all faced the same direction in the closet and none of the hangers were supposed to be touching. All his shirts had to be hung in one section; his slacks in another. (Yes, I know I promised I'd stay on track, but I can't help myself!) I didn't have many clothes of my own, or should I say many clothes that didn't have years upon years of baby spit, food, and whatever else a baby can get on a mom, and so they were all crammed at the end of the closet. Anyways, that bad habit of organizing the closet has stuck with me and I still cram my clothes at the end of the closet to make room for my husbands clothes. I hang them all in the same direction, I put the jeans or pants on the hangers all the same way, and I spread out his hangers so they don't touch. This is why my husband thinks I am a control freak. If he tries to help me with the clothes and I notice he has either hung his clothes in different ways or has crammed his hangers together then I HAVE to fix it. I can't close the closet knowing his clothes are like that. And, if by some miracle my husband manages to drag me away from the closet to ensure I leave the mess like it is then I can't sleep. I'll lay there for only so long before I have to get up and fix the darn clothes. It may seem stupid to someone who has never been abused, but it is reality for those of us who have been.

Back to Sexual Abuse I suppose... I just toggled down to read over what I had written so long ago about this form of abuse and I think I will keep most of what I wrote. I will need to do some rephrasing of it though due to my over usage of cuss words. I am learning as I go along that I am doing neither myself or anyone reading this any good when I just go off on a cuss fest in order to get my thoughts on paper. It is just so darn hard though not to want to use this forum as a way to yell at my once abuser. It is hard, but then I remind myself that our abusers don't care about what they did. They don't care, they don't care, they don't care!

Where to begin… Let me start by saying how difficult it is to have any type of physical contact with a man who does nothing but call you names, degrade you, and beat you. How are you supposed to be intimate with a monster? You get abused day in and day out, yet your abuser feels you are supposed to like his hands all over you, his mouth touching you, his manhood inside of you… (Manhood; he's no man) I don't get it. We are yelled at for not being sexy or seductive or whatever, but let's be realistic… Sex, love making, or any form of intimacy cannot be accomplished by anyone whole heartedly when they are constantly abused and ridiculed.

Sexual Abuse is our abuser's last ditch effort to take every ounce of our self- worth away from us. I am here to say it doesn't work. As with Physical Abuse, we become desensitized to what we are put through sexually by our abuser at the time it is happening. Yeah, if we are lucky enough to find a mental safe haven, we can make it through the abuse, but the after math when we are alone in the shower is devastating to our spirit. Does our abuser care, hell no. You would think our tears, lack of participation(let alone lack of AN ORGASM), and our race to get away from him once he is finished with us would be a huge indicator to our abuser that we didn't like his performance one bit, but it doesn't. We aren't seen as his loving wife or the mother of his children or even a human being for that matter. When our abusers take us sexually they only see us as , well, a hole in a tree, a piece of ass, a cum dumpster; so to speak. We are nothing to them, but a means to an end. Unfortunately that end usually is them cumming in us or on us or where ever they choose to aim it.

Sadly, I quickly came to the realization that it is better to mentally leave your body while sexual abuse is going on then it is to try to fight the tide. If you fight back or object in any way it is only worse for you and the nightmare lasts longer. I know you want to curl up and die when he is kissing you, when he is touching you, and oh dear God when he is inside of you. Unfortunately your prayers aren't answered and you have to lay there and wait for all of it to just be over. Maybe I should have written in some disclaimer stating that the views of the writer/abused are not necessarily the views of the abuser. Yes, I am being sarcastic when saying that. Of course the views of the abused are not going to be the same as the abuser; HE FEELS HE HAS DONE NOTHING WRONG!

So, the deed is done and your abuser feels he is God's gift to women and we make a mad dash to the shower. You can't imagine, or maybe you can, how many times I spent crying in the shower after he had his way with me. It is like no matter how hard you scrub you can't get his rank smell off of you, you can't wash away how he felt when he touched you, and you can't use enough soap and hot water to remove the thoughts from your mind… Just remember though that no matter what we had to endure sexually at the hands of our abusers that they were never able to take our spirit. Again, they may crush it, but they can never take it.

I know it is hard to believe me when I say our abuser, if you are being subjected to Sexual Abuse, can take only our bodies. Our soul, our minds, and our hearts will NEVER belong to them. Our abusers truly believe they have "conquered" us completely by making us endure them sexually, but they haven't conquered us and can't. Oh, don't think for a minute I didn't pray for sweet release while in the shower under that hot running water. Images of him pressing down on top of me sickened me. Still feeling like

65

his hands were groping all over me even after a long shower sickened me. Just the mere thought of his hot nasty breath on my skin sickened me. And there is no possible way; no matter how long the shower is or how hot the water; that you can rid yourself of the feeling that your abuser is still inside of you.

Sexual Abuse does not stop at just the physical contact. This abuse kind of works in reverse. If you notice, all the other forms of abuse start as head games and then escalate to physical abuse. With Sexual Abuse it starts off with all the touchy feely and then moves on to the mental fuck show. If your abuser doesn't feel he is humiliating you enough by making you endure his touch he will resort to suggesting things he wants you to do.

In my case my first husband began with telling me he wanted me to have sex with his receptionist so he could watch. I said no... He then moved on to telling me to bring home a strange woman from a bar and have sex with her while he watched. Again, I said no... He then moved on and kept suggesting he wanted me to get my best friend drunk, bring her home, and have sex with her while he watched. WHAT PART OF NO DON'T YOU UNDERSTAND? If you know I am neither a lesbian or bi-sexual then leave me alone about bringing women into our house, in front of our kids, so you can get your rocks off!!! Okay, let me just say that I neither feel lesbians and/or bi-sexual women are prone to drag strangers home in the attempts to "satisfy" the ugly hungers of their abuser. I am only stating this fact because I have a feeling I have already pissed off a few people, if they are reading this that is, and I don't need anyone else jumping the gun by misinterpreting what I am writing.

Unfortunately, this form of abuse can be done via phone as well, so even if you think you are safe because you have miles between you and your pervert of an abuser; think again... I am here to say there are no lengths our abuser won't go to to keep up the sexual abuse or should I say harassment when it inevitably comes to the phone calls (and it WILL come to the phone calls). And what made it worse for me was the fact that we have three children together, so I had to answer the stupid phone when he decided to call.

While our children and I were still living in Texas and he was with his new mistress in Florida he would call me wanting phone sex (yuck). He didn't just stop at suggesting that I do things to myself. He now wanted me to seduce one of my friend's teen aged sons and lay the phone down so he could listen. Can you believe that? If I could insert a picture of me doing the gagging thing I so totally would. It really does make me want to yack when I think about all the disgusting stuff he would say to me over the phone. Here is something for you, you pervert... I DIDN'T CARE ABOUT THE SIZE OF YOUR PENIS WHEN YOU WERE MARRIED TO ME SO WHY WOULD I CARE ABOUT IT ONCE WE WERE SEPERATED? I DON'T WANT TO "FEEL MYSELF UP" SO YOU CAN LISTEN! YOU REPULSED ME WHEN YOU WERE TOUCHING ME, SO WHAT MAKES YOU BELIEVE I'D ENJOY YOU OVER THE PHONE? CALL A 900 NUMBER FOR CRYING OUT LOUD!!!! Sorry, but I went through so much crud via phone from that man that I just want to be sick when I think about it. He even got to the point where he would hide from his new mistress/ fiancée/piggy bank in order to call me. He would lie and say he wanted to talk about the children, but then would soon change over to sex. You need some serious help if you are using our children as an excuse to try to get phone sex out of me.

The last straw was when I called him, thinking he was at work and I could leave a message, about our youngest child and he started talking about the size of his penis, that he was home alone, and he was hard. My suggestion to him? I told him I didn't care, that if his woman wasn't satisfying him that he needed to show her what to do, and that I was done hearing about his penis while I was trying to talk about the kids. I call this the last straw because as I am trying to tell him to basically F off he is on the other end of the phone masturbating; can you believe that? Has he no shame? Some people will read the above sentences and say I am just making that up to paint my ex-husband in a bad light. Those would be the same people that would also call this book a work of fiction, so I don't care about them and if you have ever been in my shoes you know all too well that I have better things to do then make up stories about my once abuser.

I can't say that I forgive my ex for all the abuse he put me through, but I can say that each day brings me closer to forgetting. There is one thing I can safely say I will neither forgive him for or forget he did to me... The day before I had to get out of his apartment he just had to prove what a "real man" he was or should I say what a "monster" he was. I had already gotten the children off to school and had to do what laundry there was to do. Yup, gotta make sure all my chores are done before I am kicked out... Anyways, he came back to the apartment for some reason before going to work. He started making advances on me and I kept refusing them. I finally stood up for myself and my body. No, it didn't work. Remember that at this point I am still wearing the hard C-collar from the neck surgery I had two months prior. He forced me stomach-side down on to the couch, ripped my shorts down, pulled me back up by wrapping his arms around my chest and hissed the following into my right ear, "You are still my wife, so you better start acting like it. I can take whatever I want"...and he did.

Throughout my entire first marriage I never truly found what it meant to be so in love with someone that you can give all of who you are to them. Now here I am, after a long road to recovery, in a loving marriage where I honestly believe sex and love making and all the fun trappings that go along with it are all mine to experience and enjoy. I went so damn long not knowing what an orgasm was that when I finally had one with my husband I couldn't stop crying. I thought I didn't deserve to feel that incredible, that I didn't deserve his love because I was damaged goods, that I didn't deserve all the pleasure love making gave me. My ex-husband had turned me into a piece of meat, his whore, and I thank God I do not feel that way about myself today.

Woohoo! We are finally on the last form of abuse I plan to cover. No, I am not cheering about the fact I get to write about yet another form of abuse. I am being sarcastic because knowing this is the last one, and I can move on to other topics, is comforting.

The last form is Ritual Abuse. I know you maybe thinking that I wrote about that earlier, but that was Religious Abuse, not Ritual. Ritual Abuse occurs mostly to women and is rarely asked or talked about. It is a form of abuse where we are subjected to ritualistic acts to pleasure our significant others. It may even be that we are forced to perform ritualistic acts on ourselves, them, or their friends. I am unable to dive any deeper into this subject since I was not a victim of this form of abuse. I cannot begin to imagine how it feels for any woman who has lived through it or is still living through it. I can hypothesize as to why our significant other (oh please, abuser) may put us through something such as this though.

For starters, if your abuser has already involved him or herself in certain types of rituals then it would only seem logical to them to have you participate in what is going on. Also, as with Sexual Abuse, it is probably your abuser's last ditch effort to take whatever part of you they have left to take, humiliate, and kill; figuratively speaking. Again, I will state this is only my hypothesis which I have drawn from the knowledge I obtained living thirteen years in an abusive relationship. I am only reiterating that little fact because I do not need a bunch of "specialists" in an uproar and shouting to the public that I have no professional background or schooling as a therapist, counselor, or psychologist and therefore should not be saying what I am. Here is my thought on THAT particular subject… Just because I didn't get paid for putting up with thirteen years of abuse does not necessarily mean I am not a "professional" nor that I didn't go through years of "schooling". I lived with a monster for thirteen plus years, so that pretty much qualifies me to say what I want when it comes to abuse! I suppose I should be delighted over the fact my first husband had no practicing religious beliefs or took part in ritualistic behavior. No beliefs of his own meant he had no reason to abuse me in that manner; thank God.

Now that I have listed the different forms of abuse, how many of you ladies have come to the realization you truly are being abused? Don't feel ashamed; you're not alone. Look at me. I had to come to the realization that out of the eight forms of abuse I covered, I was a victim of seven. But you know what; none of what I went through was my fault. that's right NONE OF IT!!! And all the crap you are having to go through everyday is not your fault either; you hearing me? So, this begs the question of whether or not we want to be domestic violence survivors or domestic violence victims.

Sorry to have to fill you in on a little secret, but that is a hard question to answer. Well, not so much to answer as it is to turn that answer into reality. We can all sit down and agree that we want to be domestic violence survivors, but it is easier said than done… I am not trying to sound like a Negative Nancy. It is just that there are so many obstacles that need to be climbed over, walked around, or barreled through before we can get our certificate proclaiming we are a "SURVIVOR". I am sure a lot of you ladies are feeling thoroughly overwhelmed right now after coming this far with me and were probably thinking our abuser was the only obstacle standing in our way on the path to freedom. I am here to say that, sadly, he is not. Unfortunately, becoming free of abuse and its after effects involves more than just getting physically away from our abuser. I am trying to think of a way to break down each obstacle so I don't get any of you reading this lost in the ramblings of my brain. Some obstacles are as obvious as the nose on our face while others creep up on us when we least expect them to or from the last places we would ever think of. Probably the best way to go about this would be to just list each obstacle, like I did the forms of abuse, and expand on each of them. I think if I do that then I will be able to stay on track and not let my thoughts wander to something else I do not want to forget to tell you.

Obstacle One: Ourselves

I bet a lot of you were thinking obstacle one would be our abuser; it's not. Crap… I am realizing I have plenty to say about this first obstacle and my brain is literally spinning a mile a minute because everything wants to be put down on paper all at the same time. Too bad I just can't lock minds with all abused women and share my thoughts simultaneously with them! That would be so like some science fiction film , wouldn't it? Are half of you now asking yourselves whether or not the gal writing all of what you are reading is playing with a full deck ? One minute I am about to discuss the obstacle of ourselves and the next minute I am talking science fiction nonsense. I am the author of this here literary masterpiece (hahahaha), so I can take a few liberties here and there I think. Maybe I shouldn't be writing today if my thoughts are running this way and that way. Though, this is my story, so why should I care if I go off on a tangent about needing coffee or make a comment here or there about things like science fiction films and locking minds with all who are reading this… Granted, this is supposed to be a book about my life during the years of abuse and what followed for me, but I am also typing what I am thinking at the moment and this means you'll have to put up with side roads. It can't all be about abuse and sadness and tears and disaster, can it? If that were all I wrote about then you'd just put down this book after reading it and swear in your hearts that there is no hope for you or anyone else being abused.

It isn't all abuse after-math and sadness and tears and disaster for me now that I am free, I promise. I just really didn't have that great of a night of sleep and all my thoughts about obstacles want to vomit themselves on to the page all at the same time. And, before you jump the gun, no my sleepless night had nothing to do with restless thoughts of past abuse running amuck through my head. It had to do with a snoring husband; God love him; and a fat fur ball of a cat that feels his place to sleep is right between my legs and up my rear. Now you know you want to laugh about that image! Alright, I am going to take a break and go surf the web for awhile. That should allow me to blow the craziness out of my brain and get focused on the first obstacle I want to talk about.

As you can see I am back and ready to jump into the topic of our first obstacle; ourselves. I say that the first obstacle we must get around is ourselves because I feel in my heart that we are our own worst enemy when it comes down to us first recognizing we are victims of abuse and, second, admitting it personally and publicly. Why is this such a difficult thing for us to do, you ask? The answer is quite simple; brainwashing.

I have been trying for the past three days now to write about this whole brainwashing deal and all I have accomplished is to type, delete, repeat. I know what I want to say, but it isn't coming out the right way; at least I don't think so. See, there is the brainwashing and then there is what happens to us when our abuser takes full advantage of said brainwashing. So, how to go about this, and make some sense of it all, is driving me a tad crazy this week. Here is my take on all of it and you can argue with me if you feel I am totally missing the mark.

We are born, and from that very day we are bombarded by older generations of women in our family that tell us we have to get married, we have to be the perfect wife, we have to be submissive, we have to "allow" our husbands certain behaviors, we have to give up dreams we want so our husband will be happy, we must do whatever it takes to make a marriage or relationship work because we don't want to be alone for the rest of our lives and so on and so on and so on.

Then if we make those same women blissfully happy by bringing children into the picture the brainwashing takes a turn and goes something like this: you need to make this marriage work for the sake of the children, you have to ignore your husband's ugliness because your children need a father, you must turn a blind eye and let things go in one ear and out the other because you can't raise children by yourself, you are just over exaggerating and things could be so much worse... Or you get the big kick to the stomach when you are told you are too hard on your husband and must be more understanding of his needs and wants. We hear this kind of crud for years upon years, so who in their right mind wouldn't call it brainwashing?

Personally I could care less about what women put up with from their men in the '20s, '30s, '40s, '50s, '60s, or '70s; whether it was the 1800s or 1900s! Sadly, this was not my philosophical belief when I was married to my first husband. As you have already read, not only was I told by my mother to let it go in one ear and out the other; I was also told repeatedly by my father that marriage was just what I saw when it came to him and my mother. If you are told and shown that women are to be the weak ones and that the men never come home or are practically in a constant state of drunkenness or go to strip clubs or never help you raise the kids or say the house is never clean enough or the cooking sucks then what on earth are you supposed to think?

Okay, so years on top of years of listening to this barbaric mentality from our family only to find a guy to marry that is the very pig you were told to love and hold on to until death do you part; woohoo! Now that we have involved ourselves with Prince Charming, he takes full advantage of how we were raised to believe a relationship works and begins his own form of brainwashing on us. I am not sure the appropriate word for our abuser is "smart", but they sure know how to use what they have heard our family members say to us and twist it into a new form of brainwashing. That is where the emotional/psychological abuse thing comes into play. Our abuser will take the very words we grew up hearing and add the ol' "don't want to disappoint your family do you" crud. So, what do we do? We don't want to disappoint our family and we surely don't want to disappoint the very man our family is in love with. We are basically screwed at this point and instead of us opening our mouths about what we are now enduring day in and day out we simply look in the mirror and try to lie ourselves into believing we have it so darn good with the man we are involved with and our family would be proud.

I can't believe I just typed that pathetic load of crap, but I was the woman standing in front of the mirror telling myself things could be worse and to not disappoint my family. Even after I went blind I still went for the mirror each morning and each night. Eventually I stopped seeing my own reflection and saw my mother's looking back at me. It was at that point I knew I was done for… Each day I went through the abuse from my first husband I still prayed that I would never turn into my mother; a woman who seemed crushed in all aspects of the word, but still married. Praying only goes so far though and eventually you have to do more than that. You have to find the strength to make your prayers a reality. How do we do this though when we have spent so many years hearing all the lies and bullshit from our family and significant other? We hear it so much and for so long we hold that to be the gospel truth and we lose sight of what is right and what is real. We are now our own worst enemy and honestly feel life is as good as it will ever get for our worthless butts and we have no one in our inner circle to tell us otherwise.

Seems pretty hopeless doesn't it? Of course it does. I lived in the land of Hopelessness for just over thirteen years, so you are not alone… What also makes our situation worse for us, and harder to open our mouths down the line, is the fact we hide or minimize the Hell we are going through to anyone who asks how we are and to ourselves. It is pounded into every cell in our bodies that we "must make it work" and that disappointing our family or man is the worst thing imaginable. This being the case we lie and lie and lie through our teeth about our life with our man. Okay, so we lie for years in order to cover up what we are going through because we don't want to feel ashamed for being a failure. Know what all those lies cause? Granted our families think all is wonderful in our world and we are making the relationship work, but it also means if we try to speak out about the abuse the odds are our family will not believe us.

Now after what I just typed how can you not believe we are the first obstacle in our way to admitting abuse? Oh, please don't think I am pushing blame on anyone who is abused because that means I am pushing blame on to myself. What I am saying though is that, unbeknownst to us, we take the words of wisdom from our families and the amplifiers heaped on those words by our abusers and end up believing it is all gold. Hell, we even take all of that and heap more falsehoods on top to ensure we do not look bad in the eyes of our families. It is like being stuck between a rock and a hard place with sand under our feet. Do we stay where we are and act like all is roses or do we start digging our way out through the very sand we are standing on? We are stuck where we are and know what to expect from family and our man, but if we start digging into the sand for what could be freedom we become scared of the unknown and feel we may suffocate to death from the sand caving in on us. It is hard, I know. We are the first obstacle and the hardest obstacle to overcome. It is possible to do though, I promise.

Obstacle Two: Getting Out of the Relationship

Hmmmm… Getting out of the nasty depths of a relationship gone wrong sounds wonderful, doesn't it? Should be really easy to pack up and leave shouldn't it? Well, it ain't! This morning I am working off of only getting two twenty minute power naps in during the last twenty-four plus hours, so I know that whatever I write from here on out will either make absolutely no sense or will be packed full of lovely cuss words and ramblings about nothing. I don't think clearly when I am overly tired and that massive chainsaw I hear from down the road is not exactly putting me in the mood to write. Some days I wish I lived way out in the sticks, so all I would hear each morning is the bird singing out my window. Though I know myself well enough to admit that after only getting in two power naps I'd be wanting to hunt that very birdie down and knock it out for being too loud… Rambling again, yes I know!

No, I have no idea why I didn't sleep last night. That's not the truth… I do know why I didn't get much sleep last night. My daughter's birthday is coming up and I am very excited for her because she is turning thirteen years old. The other reason I am not sleeping is because I am having to endure severe pelvic pain and all my primary care physician wanted to do was send me to a psychiatrist and shove numerous types of "mood behavior" pills down my throat. Pardon me, seeing I am not the doctor, but if I am having pelvic pain shouldn't I go see a gynecologist and not a shrink? If anything, I could have used a nut cracker during my first marriage when I was being beaten down physically and mentally. Look, I am taking yet another side road and rambling about the pain I am in. But, I am sure most of those reading this will be women and they will all know exactly what I mean when I say "severe pelvic pain". I could probably write a few pages on just what I thought of my primary doctor and that whole appointment with him, but it is so far out there that many would think I was making it up for a good laugh. So, I will depart from that topic and bid you ladies farewell so I can get some needed sleep. Once I have accomplished that then I'll be able to write and stay on track.

I got the desperately needed sleep with a three hour long nap this morning. I am also happy to report there is no more chainsaw blaring from down the way. The pain is still there though and is not much of a help. I did go over what I wrote earlier though and noticed I used the phrase nut cracker. So, in using that term; how many psychiatrists or psychologists or therapists or counselors did I offend? Am I sorry for using the term, no. I suppose though I should watch what I say before someone screams that I am not politically correct; whatever that means these days. Let's get back to the topic of getting out of the relationship we have finally admitted has gone severely wrong.

As I have said, "it is easier said then done". Oh sure, we can finally admit to ourselves that "I've got to get out, I've got to leave, I'm gonna do it I swear", and I am sure the first handful of times you said it to yourself in your head, or while looking at your reflection in the mirror, you truly believed you were going to leave. Let's get real though; you won't leave. I fought that inner battle with myself. I know darn well what it is like to break down and cry, swear you had enough, and pick up the phone; you're not alone.

We know in the depths of our soul that each day we allow to pass by without getting out of the toxic relationship we are in is wrong, wrong, wrong… but we are forgetting two things; the devil sitting on our right shoulder and the devil sitting on our left shoulder. I know some of you are probably trying to correct me by saying an angel sits on our right shoulder and a devil sits on our left; not in our case. The devil on our right is our loving family who knows better than we do and our left shoulder is home to the devil of our abuser. We finally get up the courage to admit, even if just to ourselves, that we are victims of domestic violence only to find once we have done that those little devils pop up on our shoulders to knock us back down to the ground. As I have already stated; we are stuck between a rock and a hard place while standing on a floor of sand. Our abuser knows this and those little bastards sitting on our shoulders know this.

Once we have admitted what we are and what our relationship has turned into we feel like we can take on the world, but as soon as we start digging in the sand for a way out those lovely devils begin to whisper in our ears. They whisper that we can't leave because we have no where to go. They whisper that we are worthless and no one would want our tainted selves. They whisper that we'll never truly escape the relationship. They whisper that keeping the family together is best for everyone. They whisper that we couldn't possibly take the children and raise them alone. They whisper we are too weak to stand up for ourselves. They whisper and whisper and whisper every nasty little thing we have heard over the years until we cry defeat and stop trying to dig our way to freedom.

So, we listen to all the madness whispered in our ears by mere figments of our imagination; our invisible chains; and we stop believing we are victims of domestic violence and that we need to get out. It is sad to admit that in a way we get used to being treated like a bag of garbage, a piece of shit, a speck of dirt, a wad of gum stuck to the bottom of our abuser's shoe and that going out into the unknown scares us more than a slap to the face or a round of mental pistol whipping. I mean come on, with a slap to the face we already know it is coming, how hard it will hurt, what damage it will cause and we've heard just about every ugly thing another human being can spit at us; what's a little more gonna do? If we pack our bags and head for a new life we have no fricking idea what to expect. It is this fear that makes us cling to the life we are living; no matter how pathetic or horrible it may be. So, please don't read these sentences and feel you are the only victim of domestic violence that was too scared to leave, but too scared to stick around. You are not alone in this internal struggle.

Common sense tells us what we are going through day in and day out is wrong, but with every slap, punch, nasty word, or other mental trashing of us, we are made to feel there is nothing better out there in the world. I am here to say that there is more for you out there in the great unknown though, so much more. Oh, it isn't an easy road to travel, but the end result is so worth it! I thought I would never recover and that what my abuser had been putting me through was better then what I was enduring at the time, but that all changed with time and I sometimes kick myself for not getting out years sooner. Crud, I was on a writing high only to be tossed down just now by a lovely chainsaw again; grrrr. I'll unfortunately have to stop for this morning and start in with obstacle three tomorrow morning. Stupid chainsaw…

Obstacle Three: Our Abuser

So, you have accomplished the hard task of getting around the first two obstacles; hooray! Pat yourselves on the back ladies because those were hard obstacles to get through. The obstacle you are about to encounter now though is more of a life road block that mirrors your every move. It is the stain on the carpet that you can never get rid of no matter how hard you try. It is the cockroach you swore you had exterminated only to find it in your kitchen the next day. It is the drip from the bathroom sink that is there one day, gone the next, and back again. It is our abuser and he has absolutely no intentions of letting us go any time soon. Sure, you made it out of the house you dwelled in with him, but he still wants that hold over you, that control, and it's not going to sink into his skull that you are not coming back. See, we know we have managed to remove the stamp that says we are "The Property of Jackass", but he hasn't figured that out for himself yet.

This lovely next obstacle is not just a physical one, it is also a psychological one. I had to delete what I wrote yesterday about this because in reading it I realized it was a bunched up mess. See, there is the tangibly real aspect of this obstacle and then there is the part that is purely psychological and I need to break the two apart and talk about them individually. Unfortunately, for any lady that has been in our shoes, the psychological part is just as real. To any outsider though, that has never experienced what we have, the psychological part is completely in our heads and a pretty little pill will fix that problem.

Sorry other people, but shoving pills down our throats is not the way to rid ourselves of the psychological aspect of this obstacle. All pills do is put us in a jacked up haze and what kind of life is that? Oh, I am sure the drug companies would love for thousands upon thousands of battered women to line up outside their doors and request a Happy Pill. Here is the kicker to your Happy Pill Fixes All theory. If the underlying problem of, oh I don't know… ABUSE, is not addressed then that Happy Pill turns into a bedside table full of various Happy Pills or a medicine cabinet that looks like your local pharmacy. Eventually all of those pills don't work, and the chances are, the Happy Pills are joined by anything that can be drank, snorted, shot up, or smoked. So yeah, I guess I don't care for Happy Pills or shrinks or twelve step programs or condescending family members!

I can't stop sneezing for some reason and it is making typing, let alone thinking straight, a tad difficult (side road, I know). Hold on and let me see if blowing my nose will help any. Good thing we aren't face to face while all this sneezing is going on. I bet my monitor looks nice and wet about now, but I refuse to stop typing in order to cover my mouth. Oh please, how many of you have sneezed and neglected to cover your mouth? It is just that when I am on a roll, I don't like stopping for much of anything; okay, except for coffee... I am only human and therefore not even close to perfect, so quit mumbling to yourself about my bad habits!

Alright, I am back and my coffee is stone cold; yuck. I am still not completely clear on how to separate the physical part of this obstacle and the psychological part. They are both very real to me, or were, and there is a side of me that feels it is utterly important not to minimize what we go through once we have left an abusive relationship. Life is not always neat and pretty and this happens to be one of those times. I want to think about this for awhile longer. I want to do this right and get all of it out. I know the writing isn't coming difficult to me because I am still dealing with this obstacle. I think the issue is that this one does play a mental fuck show on those of us who go through it and I really need to convey that to anyone reading this.

Well, taking yesterday to think about this subject did me no good. To be honest with you I really have no idea why I am sitting in front of the computer right now trying to discuss this obstacle with you. I still have no idea how to break apart the two aspects of this obstacle. Maybe I shouldn't think at all about it and just write whatever pops into my head. Problem with that? Well, all that is coming to my mind are flashbacks of what I went through and sorry, but this is not a picture book… Know what I think? Ha, of course you don't. I think what I will do is expand on what I wrote earlier when I called our abuser the stain in the carpet that won't go away, the cockroach in the kitchen, and the drip that is there one minute and gone the next. I called our abuser those things for a reason when it comes to him being an obstacle, so that is how I will approach this topic. I am not saying that each woman experiences all of the aforementioned descriptions of their abuser once she has gotten out of the relationship, but I am saying she has probably at least experienced one.

First let's talk about the stain in the carpet that won't go away no matter how hard you scrub and scrub and scrub at it. That oh so lovely stain will appear in a multitude of places and be the most annoying thing ever. Picture this, if you will… Isn't that an opening line from one of those black and white back in the day science fiction television shows? I am sure it would appear by now that I am some sort of science fiction freak or nerd or geek, but I will chalk it up to being married to a man who dares to dream of the unknown while I keep my feet firmly planted on the ground. (Focus, lady, focus.)

Okay, we have escaped our abuser and have started to establish our new home miles and miles away from him. We are finally feeling safe and comfortable, and are actually bordering on the on ramp to happiness, when all of a sudden there is a knock at our front door. Why the knock? We just moved in and aren't expecting any company or deliveries… Unfortunately, there is no peep hole or window with a clear view of the front door or God forbid we are BLIND, so we have no choice but to open the door. Looky, looky; it is the recurring carpet stain. He wants to come in, he wants to talk, he wants us back, he wants to make things work, he will do anything if we just "come home". So, what do we do? We know if we piss him off by standing our ground; which by the way is not firm yet; then he just might push his way into our new place and within a matter of minutes turn us into the cowering dog whose tail is between its legs. We also know if we attempt to appease him he will take us for still being weak and try to take major advantage of that. So, what are we supposed to do? There is no right answer for that question and, sadly, we who have been abused will all pick different ways to get rid of our abuser and they will all be the wrong choice. I say they will all be the wrong choice only because our abusers are messed up mentally and cannot be reasoned with. They are on your new front door step for one reason and one reason only; to get their punching bag back under their roof.

It isn't just your front door though where the stain reappears. His task is to regain control and he needs to prove he is omnipresent in the new life you are trying to establish for yourself. What does this all mean? This means you will see him outside the grocery store you like to shop at, he'll be outside the place that has decided to hire you, he will follow you when you are doing errands, and you might even find him out by your post box. I literally have chills writing about this because I had to live it. I had to live with the fear of never knowing if my abuser was around or not. I guess that is the worst thing about being blind and being a survivor of abuse. I don't think anyone reading this could possibly understand the depths of my fear fully though unless they heard me speak about it all.

What makes our abuser "smart" during all of this stalking is that he has made sure that no one in your new town sees him with you or near you. He has made sure he has blended in with the surroundings like any John Smith in the neighborhood. He is there one minute and gone the next and the only one who knows is you. Once our abuser feels he has made his point of being omnipresent he will more than likely fade out of sight in order to give you a false sense of security. One day he is all up in your face about wanting you back and the next he is telling you he will leave you alone and stay out of your life. THAT IS SUCH A LOAD OF CRAP!!! What is so pathetic about that is we so desperately want for that load of crap to be true and we fall for it. We manage to go a few days, then weeks, then maybe a month without seeing our abuser anywhere, so we feel that maybe just maybe this time he meant what he said and he will leave us alone; HA!

This is when our abuser turns away from being the stain in the carpet to becoming the cockroach we thought we had exterminated... I am sorry if what I am writing is making anyone reading this feel defeated and that there is absolutely no way out of the abusive maze they are in. I just feel it is important for you ladies to know what you could possibly be up against while traveling down the road to freedom. Here it is in front of you in black and white; no sugar coating, no one telling you it is all in your head. So, as I said a few lines ago we manage to go awhile without seeing our abuser and we are beginning to get that false sense of security he is hoping we get. Then what? Well, then we leave the store one day to find him out in the parking lot standing next to our car or we take a walk through the park to discover him sitting on a bench with newspaper in hand or we go to check our mail only to see him parked down the street. Why is he doing this you wonder? He is doing this to remind us that we really aren't safe in our new town, our new house or apartment, our new life. We thought, like the cockroach we exterminated, that we got rid of him because he "lied" and said "he would leave", but there he is and now we are yet again living in fear. We are unwillingly involved in our abuser's sick game to drive us mental; great...

It doesn't end with seeing our abuser every so often here or there though. He'll do a slue of other things to remind us that he has not given up on controlling us or the situation. So, not only do we have to worry about our abuser popping up out of nowhere, but we also have to deal with unwanted emails, unwanted letters in the post, and unwanted phone calls in the middle of the night. Not that we want to have to deal with endless phone calls during the day, but he'll slip some in during the late hours of the night in hopes to wake you up or "catch" you with another man or whatever his disturbed mind has conjured up to be reality. It is sick, I know, but it is the truth. This part of the obstacle or roadblock gets so bad that we dread checking our email, we dread checking the post, and all we want to do is shut our cell phones or landlines off in order to stop the ringing! This is also the point in our abuser's sick game where he has us so messed up mentally that we are beginning to question whether or not if what we saw, heard, or smelled was real or a figment of our imagination. Our abuser has harassed us, tormented us, and stalked us to the point we begin to feel he is all around us; he is everywhere; we'll never be truly free. We begin to question our own mental stability and so do those around us.

When it gets this far then our abuser has successfully gone from being the cockroach to being the drip in the bathroom sink. I use this phrase to describe our abuser because like the drip in the sink he is there one minute, gone the next, and the thought of him/it reappearing makes you cringe. It is pure torture to go through this part of our journey to recovery. I know what I want to say, but really don't know where to start. I got through my abuser being the carpet stain and even through him being the cockroach, but the part where he was the drip in the sink seemed to last forever for me and I only get chills thinking about that span of time. It is no joke that you begin to question yourself; what you saw, what you heard, what you smelled. Yup, I said, "what you smelled". If your abuser has successfully made it to the status of the drip in the sink then you will start developing triggers. Well, not so much you developing them as much as one could say they begin to take form. Triggers range from hearing a car drive by that sounds just like the one your abuser drives to smelling the smoke from the same cigar or cigarette that your abuser smokes to a particular cologne your abuser wears to a nearby ringtone you hear in the store or parking lot that happens to be the same ringtone you have for your abuser on your very own cell phone.

Granted, these triggers are caused by folks who have no idea they are even doing it, but they are still there and nag us for an immediate gut response to the stimuli. Sadly, this generally means we feel sick to our stomach or we break out in a cold sweat or we begin to feel we are not safe unless we lock ourselves in our place of residence. Even then we don't feel truly safe because we cannot block out all the triggers and we cannot be for sure anymore which ones are honestly the cause of our abuser and which ones aren't. Hell, we even start hearing the ringtone or vehicle or whatever in our sleep. So, then sleep isn't even a safe haven from our abuser. I know it sounds wicked hopeless to get out of this stage of our recovery, but it will happen if you take a few necessary steps.

Before I take the chance of getting in trouble from some expert with letters following their name let me just say this... The steps I am about to mention were only tested and proven effective for my specific case. You do what you have to do to maintain mental stability and a grasp on your new found life. So, here is what I did to be proactive in my attempts at a normal, abuse-free future.

-I started by filling my home with my favorite scent until my senses no longer remembered what my abuser's cologne smelled like, what our old house/apartment smelled like, what the laundry smelled like.
-I changed my ringtone on my cell phone to one I knew most people would not have and to remind myself what a "King of all Excuses" he was.

-I began forcing myself to listen to passing vehicles until they eventually all sounded alike. This one was hard since I am blind. I wanted to vomit each time I thought I heard his truck, but I repeatedly told myself my abuser had done his worst and it was only a car passing by.

-I slowly began changing the schedule I was forced to follow out of fear and fell into my own routine. This meant leaving a dirty glass in the kitchen sink or tossing a pair of dirty jeans somewhere other than the hamper or throwing down my tennis shoes where ever I took them off. Alright, I'll admit I was not always successful at this part, and I still fight with the old routine, but I am getting much better at it.

-I surrounded myself with people which taught me not to be afraid of being in public. This meant getting over the fear that all males were evil and would abuse me if given the chance. For a long time my brother was the only guy I felt safe around. If we keep up this line of thought though we will never find a real man, a true man, that can love us like we deserve to be loved.

-I bought furniture that my first husband would have turned his nose up to. This was very liberating since he was the one who got to pick out all the furniture for thirteen years.

These were just the major things I did to overcome the triggers. It took me a long time to be able to handle being alone with anyone (even the pizza delivery guy), a long time to overcome the fits of shaking like a Chihuahua, a long time before I stopped hearing a ringtone that wasn't there, a long time before I wasn't afraid of my own shadow; so to speak… God, it seemed like it took so much darn time… Even if your abuser is not all up in your face he will relish in the thoughts that you are miserable in your new life, your new home, your new skin. Fight back ladies, fight back!

Obstacle Four: Kicked Dog Syndrome

With any addiction there is a risk of a relapse. Yes, I just said addiction… I am sure many folks would say there is no chance that a woman who is a victim of domestic violence could possibly become addicted to it, but I am here to say we can.

Take a look at most addictions. They're not good for us, we know they are not good for us, and yet we keep going back to them. Drugs, alcohol, cigarettes, caffeine, chocolate… it is all addicting and all bad for our health in the long run. Our abuser is the same as any drug or bottle of alcohol or pack of cigarettes or any amount of caffeine or endless bars of chocolate. We might be able to quit the crap for awhile, but we all get sucked back into it for one reason or another. Drugs, alcohol, cigarettes, caffeine, and chocolate all make us feel good for the moment or make us forget our pain, if only for a little while, or calm our nerves. We all end up hating ourselves though for being weak and succumbing to our addiction, but we do it anyway.

Please don't misunderstand me and what I just said. I am not saying that our addiction to our abuser gives us the same chemical effect or rush that the above mentioned items do. What I am saying is that we know in our hearts our abuser is bad for us, but there is a part of us that truly believes if we just give into him then the torment will stop, the pain will stop, the madness will stop. Oh, we know a relapse is bad for us, but we can't help it. I call this the "Kicked Dog Syndrome" or KDS. Sad to say there is no quick fix for this problem!

For those who are still in denial that you are a victim of domestic violence and swear you have no darn idea what I am talking about I will make myself clear. Those of us who find themselves in an abusive relationship that has spanned across years and years end up developing KDS when we finally try to leave the relationship. It varies in degree from woman to woman, but we basically all have it. I call it KDS because just like the dog that is repeatedly kicked by its owner, only to come back to it, so do we with our abuser. Please don't confuse the term KDS with us being the cowering dog. They may seem the same, but are not. The cowering dog in us KEEPS us in the toxic relationship of abuse and tries to knock us off the path of recovery while KDS develops after we leave, and tries its damnedest to suck us back in. So there is no chance of me losing anyone I will list a few of the signs that you can look for to determine if you have KDS or not. I have a feeling though once you have read the list that follows there will be a lot of you who will have to admit to yourselves that you have been a party to them even after you thought you were done with all of it.

-responding to his every email
-responding to each of his phone calls
-letting him into your new place -meeting "just to talk" and end up having sex with him
-letting him move back in
-letting him con you into moving back in
-loaning him money you will never see repaid
-letting him borrow your vehicle
-listening to him whine and cry about wanting to make things work
-believing him when he lies about wanting to make things work
-contacting him IN ANY WAY while in a moment of weakness

And the list goes on and on and on. Believe me when I say it will never stop unless you grow a spine and stand your ground. Remember ladies, this is all about control for our abuser. Control, control, control… As long as you believe in your heart you are the door mat your abuser has repeatedly treated you like you were then you will always have Kicked Dog Syndrome!

I sat back and watched my abuser move out, move back in, move out, and move back in. I put up with my abuser telling me I was worthless. I paid thousands upon thousands of dollars to my abuser and haven't seen a dime of it back. Even after he kicked me out I put up with his constant harassing phone calls, his emails, his lies; all of it. Why? Well, I think after thirteen years of abuse I was just so damned used to it that I knew nothing else. I knew I didn't want him in my life because he was my abuser, a cancerous disease, but I still put up with his shit and for what… I had absolutely no moral obligation to my abuser. I knew he would never change. I knew he was the cause of all the negativity in my life. I knew I would never truly heal if I allowed him to keep his invisible leash on me.

So, then why put up with it? You are not alone if you find yourself asking that very same question. Here I was on the highway to freedom and I was making constant U-turns and heading back towards the very car wreck I was trying to get away from. It is a nasty and vicious cycle we ladies go through when experiencing KDS, no doubt about it. What is that thing in the solar system that sucks objects into it? Oh, a Black Hole… That is exactly what our abuser is; a Black Hole that sucks us in with such force that it takes us repeated attempts to free ourselves from its gravitational pull and our inevitable death!

I am going to take another side road for awhile. First off, I haven't typed a single word for about the last two months due to self-pity. Yes, even I suffer from self-pity. Surprisingly, it has nothing to do with the topic of this loosely written book. I am dealing with female medical problems, which I referred to earlier, and all of the pain and discomfort was really getting to me. I am still dealing with the female issues, but am refusing to let them run or rule my day to day goings on. Eventually there will come a second opinion and probably surgery, but until then I'll forge on. Second, I am taking this side road because something has been happening lately that concerns my three children and their father. I am not sure if you could put this situation under the forms of abuse I discussed earlier or under obstacles in our way while we walk the path to recovery. In a way I think it is a little of both and I hope my thoughts are collected in a manner to which; once typed out; you will understand them.

My children's father is attempting to brainwash our oldest child (a boy) and is making empty promises to our children. It is actually more than that. In doing these other things he Is hoping to manipulate and control me or at least get our oldest son to. I realize because of the current situation I cannot shield any of my children from the lies and venom their father spits out on a daily basis in order to get himself higher on the food chain, but at this point I can't even diminish its effects on at least our oldest boy. I understand my son is now fourteen years old and is told he is a young man, but if he is truly the young man his father tells him he is, then his father should not feel the need to try to brainwash him or control his every move. See, I am rambling and not explaining things as well as I should.

Okay, let me try this route. I have a good relationship with my children's paternal grandfather because we both put the kids first. This fact pisses off my ex-husband to no end and he is constantly telling our oldest son that my relationship with the father he disowned ages ago is wrong. This means every time I visit or talk with my kids my oldest son has been throwing this in my face. Throwing it in my face is too harsh of a phrase to use. Let's say that our oldest son keeps bringing up the topic of his paternal grandfather, me, that whole relationship, and how it upsets his father. I have told my oldest son how relationships work and that I keep a good one with his grandfather for the sake of them. I also try to bring to light the lies his father tells him and what his father conveniently chooses to omit about the whole relationship that does not exist between him and his biological father. My oldest son used to listen and decide for himself, but now is calling the one person; me; that doesn't lie to him a liar. I know our oldest son feels incredibly torn. I know he is constantly bombarded on a regular basis with negative things being said about me and his paternal grandfather. I know it is hard for him and I do not blame him for anything he says. Our oldest son is coming to conclusions about things based solely on what his father's side of the family says. That side of the family is, I'm sure, a great influence... A great negative one as far as I am concerned, but what can I do except clean up the mess once it is all over. There will come a day when our oldest son realizes I tell the truth about things because I have absolutely nothing to lose. His father and his relatives see lying as a way to keep a hold on what they feel is theirs to lose. Love is not a God-given right. We can't assume lies and manipulation will force our children to love us. This is a concept I do not feel my ex-husband will ever grasp.

I had several lines typed up, but just went back to delete them. I was rambling about something that, honestly, is worth a book of its own. I guess what it all boils down to is this... The abuse you endured will only linger if there are children involved. Our children become unwilling pawns and you are diluting yourself if you think, even for a second, that your abuser won't try to taint the minds of your children. It just becomes an extension of the control our abusers refuse to relinquish. Nothing is sacred... not even the well-being of our children. It is this little dose of reality that saddens me today.

What else is getting my goat is a line my first husband has decided to use repeatedly in emails to me. I am paraphrasing here, but it goes something like this, "Let's put aside our anger for the sake of the kids". Why is it so damn easy for the abuser to suggest that we "put aside our anger"? Does he honestly say that with a straight face? Of course it is easy for the one dishing out the abuse to suggest setting aside the anger; he isn't being abused, controlled, or manipulated!!! Here our abuser is, pretty much on a daily basis, trying to go to any lengths necessary to keep a hold on us. Even after we are out of the abusive relationship, our abuser will con himself into believing he has that magical hold on us like he used to. I know darn well that if any abuser has the stupidity to use this phrase on us, it is only because they want something. An abuser does nothing unless he believes it will benefit him in the long run. If he didn't care about you when he was abusing you, and couldn't set aside his anger for the sake of the kids then, then why would he put it aside now? Unbelievable! Sometimes I feel my ex-abuser is a true idiot, but he gives me constant material to talk about with you ladies. I know I am not the only woman whose ex-husband or boyfriend or significant other thinks the sun rises and sets for him and him alone.

Alright, enough said about that subject. I am sure I will have more to write about it in the months to come. I feel like my life belongs on one of those daytime talk shows that portray everyone as trailer trash with nothing higher than a seventh grade education! I don't watch daytime TV, so are those types of shows even on anymore? Goodness knows my temperament towards the past with my ex is not refined enough for Ms. O and Lord knows there is no way my ex-abuser would consent to having Ms. O knock him down a few rungs by interviewing him! HAHAHAHAHAHAHAHAHAHAHAHAHAHA, that would be hilarious... One abuser against a studio audience full of empowered women who refuse to put up with crap. I could pee myself from laughter!!!

I really should get back on track when it comes to the obstacles we end up facing and, hopefully, conquering. I did have Obstacle Five as the in-laws or soon to be ex-in- laws or finally ex- in-laws, but maybe I should write about our own family members first. When we are going through the madness of being abused, I don't think it ever really crosses our minds that once we decide to stand up for ourselves and leave, there would be any member of our family who would try to impede our efforts, but sadly it does happen. Hmmm, which one to tackle first... I think I will go after the in-laws first, only because most times our abuser keeps us from our own family and close to his.

Obstacle Five: The In-laws

There are two types of in-laws that I am aware of, the blackmailers and the spies. If there is an in-law of the third kind out there I'd be hard pressed to find them! Let me explain myself better, so I do not rub any in-laws the wrong way. If you are involved in an abusive relationship, then you run the risk of having one of the two types I am about to discuss. If you are not involved in an abusive relationship, then the types of in-laws you may encounter will range from wonderful to horrid. We are not covering those types of in-laws though. Thankfully, my current husband's ex-wife was nothing to write home about, and therefore it didn't take much for me to "raise the bar" with his mom; hahahaha! Granted, if we end up married, we run the risk of having the stereotypical in-laws that feel we are never good enough for their son or something along those lines. Things change though once they acknowledge what is truly going on or become aware of the fact that you see their perfect son is nothing more than an abusive monster. They either turn into The Blackmailers or The Spies. I was fortunate enough (if you can use that term) not to have the Blackmailer in-laws, but do know of ladies who have had to put up with this type.

The Blackmailer in-law is the kind who will do whatever it takes to keep you in a relationship with their son. Why, you ask. Isn't it obvious? If they can get you to stick it out with their son then they don't have to deal with him. Oh, and if grandchildren are involved then the in-laws will go to enormous lengths to keep you with their son. Heaven forbid your unhappiness comes in the way of them seeing the grandchildren. This is really turning my stomach this morning. I don't like having to admit I know there are people in this world that are like the ones I am describing! I truly don't understand ugliness in another person, so that sort of behavior boggles my mind. If that means people will see me as naïve to the "ways of the world", then I'd sooner be known as naïve rather then someone with an abusive personality.

Back on track though. As I was saying, they will go to most any lengths to keep you involved with their son. What does this include? Well, at first your soon-to-be in- laws will accept you into the family like you are the greatest thing since sliced bread. Your in-laws will treat you like you were their own daughter, lavish you with gifts and loving words, and try to blow over any hint of ugliness you might see in their son. It is like a sweet and sappy Sugar Fest. All the attention they heap on you, prior to you even marrying their son, is just the spider (them) luring the fly (you) into their web. See, this type of in-law already knows what a nightmare their boy is. They are just hoping all the "love" they smother you with will blind you to that dose of reality.

So, they have successfully bribed you into sticking it out with their son and you are now hitched to your abuser; 'til death do you part. Time goes by though and the Blackmailing in-law is not so sweet and sappy because their son is now your problem. Now if you show discontent for their son, and they find out, they will begin to do little things to appease you. Well, got a late notice because the electric bill wasn't paid? No worries the loving in-laws will pay that little bill for you. Behind on your rent for the month? Think nothing of it, the in-laws will take care of that too. I could go on and on. You need a car in order to work, so your lazy man can stay home? Just mention it to your in-laws and BAM, there is a car in your drive. It may not be the prettiest of vehicles, Lord knows the in-laws don't want to break the bank, but it runs and passed inspection. Need groceries? Oh goodness, let the in-laws help. They can't bear knowing one of their grandchildren are going without.

So now what? Well, at first all of this help you were getting from your in-laws made them look like saviors, I am sure, but months upon months have gone by and now they let you know that strings have always been attached. What does this all mean? It means it is time to pay the piper and the price is staying with your in-laws abusive son. If you think for one minute you are going to walk out that front door with their grandchildren, and leave their nightmare of a son, then you have another thing coming! They didn't pay off your bills here and there or pick up that gallon of milk or get you a half-decent car just so your ungrateful behind could walk away from their son!

Of course they know you aren't the total reason the bills are late or there is no food in the house or their grandchildren aren't dressed to the nines, but that doesn't stop them from saying you are. Admitting their son is abusive or lazy or actually the worthless piece of shit he constantly calls you would be a reflection on them as parents and the blackmailing type in-law can't have that. What would the neighbors say? So, if the in-laws begin to feel their "helping hand" approach won't keep you with their son then they will try another one. Your in-laws will turn from being your saviors to being the ones who will make sure their son has an attorney that will rip you apart in court and take away your children. Some of you ladies know exactly what I am talking about, don't you? For any woman who has had to endure years of abuse and then found themselves having to deal with these kind of in-laws... I am truly sorry.

On to the other type of in-law; great... This type of in-law is The Spy. I had the misfortune of having this very type and will probably talk more about this kind later on in the book. How do I define the Spy in-law, hmmm. For starters this type of in-law also already knows what a monster their son is, but blood is thicker than water or any moral high ground, so beware! The Spy in-laws won't go out of their way to help you financially or blackmail you in any round about way. Heck, the odds are they will be sweet as honey to your face and then bash you to the rest of the family as soon as they think you aren't in ear shot. Their main focus is to "befriend" you in order to keep tabs on you. They will gain your trust and give you a false sense that you have their complete confidence and full understanding. I am here to scream at the top of my lungs that these in-laws are despicable in my eyes. They find it totally acceptable to lie to you and manipulate you with any means necessary. What is the point of this twisted behavior? I am starting to go off track here, sorry. I need to take a long, deep breath and collect the thoughts I want to put on paper and put my ugly thoughts about this subject into a mental envelope for another day.

Who am I kidding! I have been up since before 2:00 AM and everything I wrote above is making no sense to me. Okay, that is not completely true. It makes total sense to me, but is coming off a bit bitchy. I think you ladies know by now that I cannot bring myself to write about something unless I am in the mood to do so and feel I am writing it in a way that is helpful. I did not set out to write this loosely called book in order to have a platform for my bitchiness and I know that what I was inevitably going to write about my ex-in-laws would have read like a personal attack. Granted, it would have been a justifiable personal attack, but that sort of thing can wait. Just as we need to scream out how we feel about our abuser in order to recover; we also must about our in-laws. If you look back and analyze it, they abused us too, in their own sadistic way… I can just imagine my ex's mother shaking an index finger at this very moment and saying, "Shame on you!" (already been down that road).

I wanted to deal with the Spy in-law stuff because it was the next phase of my book. Nothing is flowing though, which makes getting my point across virtually impossible. My solution to this problem? I will leave the in-laws behind, for now, and move on to something else. When I have purged myself of what my inner-self feels it needs to talk about, then I'll go back to discussing the in-laws and any other obstacle I believe stands in our way to recovery.

I think all the editing and reformatting I am doing with this book has forced me off the path of why I was writing it in the first place. (Yup, I am having to deal with editing and formatting issue; something I "just love") I was losing my focus and it led me to being nothing more than a hamster running in circles on its exercise wheel. Know what I mean? So, in order to remedy that I am going to share something with you ladies that I have shared with no one. Part of my recovery, and letting it out/letting it go, was to make a journal of my abuse; a history, if you will. I started from the beginning, wrote the approximate date (if not the actual date), wrote the city/state I was living in at the time, and what I had to endure. Regurgitating it all back on to the page, and out of my head, was insanely therapeutic! Even though it was a good thing for me to do; it was also bittersweet. I had to relive it all, but I didn't cry like I thought I would. Then, when I read it all back, it only reconfirmed my position that NONE OF IT WAS MY FAULT! I highly recommend to all of you who are, or were, involved in an abusive relationship to make a journal of what you have had to endure. If there is any woman still in doubt as to whether or not they are being abused, even after I listed the forms of abuse, will think again after seeing their abuse in print. So, here goes ladies… my history of abuse.

January 31, 1993-Brutus/Petoskey, MI.

It was Super Bowl time; Dallas Cowboys vs. Buffalo Bills. Even though my ex's favorite team is the Steelers, he holds a place in his heart for the Bills. We were at my grandparents home watching the game and Dallas made an exceptionally good play, which I made the mistake of commenting on. My comment was followed up by my ex yelling at me about knowing nothing about football; that I wasn't a loyal fan; that I rooted for whatever team was winning; that I was stupid. Dallas won 52 - 17 and my ex just kept up with the yelling. On the car ride back to our college dorms he continued to yell the same crap at me; how I knew nothing about football or how to be a loyal fan and how I needed to keep my fucking mouth shut. Instead of pulling into the dorm parking lot, he pulled into the campus parking lot and turned off the car. There he kept me for over a half an hour just yelling at me about that one comment I made. I sat there thinking, "how does anyone get this mad over a football game?". I learned not to say a single thing about football after that night.

August 1993-Monroe, MI.

I was getting ready for work and an argument started about our families. I just began working for a local shopping super center after finding out I was not getting paid a dime for all the hours I had been working at my in-laws deli/yogurt shop. He followed me into his parents kitchen yelling about how my family sucked and how I needed to keep my mouth shut about his family. He ended up shoving me down a set of stairs leading from his parents' kitchen to the mudroom. I got outside and walked myself over a mile to work. Once at work my co-worker noticed red marks across my neck and cheek. She took me upstairs to where we kept the layaway to look at my back for any bruising from being shoved down the stairs. My ex called me at work to yell at me and tell me I had better not have told anyone what he had done to me. His step-father picked me up after work that night and just said, "Things will get better."

October 1993-Pennsylvania.

An argument started again about how my family sucked and I had better shut up about his family; that I knew nothing about them. He pushed me into his cousin's bedroom closet, which was full of junk, and proceeded to shove and slap me around. I was pinned against the wall and floor of the closet while he was doing this. I punched him in the chest to get him off of me. I ended up with three of my upper left ribs out of whack. I never went to the doctor; it just hurt so bad to breathe. I still get pain in them once in awhile and you can feel the difference between those three ribs and the rest of the ones I have. I learned quickly that standing up for myself just made my punishment worse.

December 1993-Gaines, MI.

We were now staying with my parents after we were kicked out of his aunt's house. An argument started in my parents' living room about, what else, family. Again, my family sucked and I was told I knew nothing about his family and needed to keep my fucking mouth shut. I tried to get away from him shoving and slapping me by walking towards the bedroom at the back of the house. He followed me and while in the hallway, grabbed the back of my neck, twisted up my necklace in his fist and ripped it off. He managed to choke me with it before it broke off and then proceeded to push me down on to the floor of the hallway. While there, he pinned me down on my stomach and told me to never say another word about his family.

February 1994-Brutus, MI.

My ex received a packet in the mail that he opened up in my grandparents driveway. I asked him what it was about, and after reading it, he got angry. The letter was from the court informing him of his recent adoption and his legal last name would be White unless he showed up in court to dispute the name White on his birth certificate. I again asked him about it because I knew, while we lived in Monroe, MI, that his mother was constantly riding him about allowing her third husband to adopt him. I had been told, repeatedly, that he was not about to let his mother control him or force him into signing anything when it came to being adopted (being on the verge of turning23, mind you). Reminding him of those conversations only pissed him off more. After being told to mind my fucking business, he took the packet, shoved it under the left rear wheel-well panel in the trunk, and then traded in the Escort for a Probe. I was told never to speak of the paperwork to anyone.

February 1994-Brutus, MI.

I was getting ready for work and my ex started yelling at me about family and money. I stupidly told him to shut up because we were staying with my grandparents, rent free, and I was tired of his yelling at me. He answered that by punching me repeatedly in the right arm. He instantly left bruises that stretched from my shoulder to just above my elbow. I had short sleeved uniforms and the bruising couldn't be hidden. While driving me to work he continued to yell at me; shoving and punching the left side of my head, so that the right side of my head would slam into the car window as he drove. He kept yelling that I needed to hide the bruises and keep my mouth shut about how I got them. I couldn't hide the bruises and the girls training with me saw them. I told both of them how I got the bruises and begged them to not say anything to the nurses on our floor.

April 1994-Brutus, MI.

While driving into Petoskey for groceries we started arguing about family. Again, he told me how my family sucked and that I better not say a word about his. He also yelled at me for being a lazy worthless piece of shit. I argued back about the fact that I had a job and was bringing in money. He just kept yelling and then started punching me in the left side of my head; forcing me to press my head against the car window. He eventually found a patch of road, that was in the middle of no where, and pulled over. He just kept yelling and punching me. I tried to leave the car, but where he had stopped put my door up against a snow bank and my door wouldn't open much. Once in Petoskey, he pulled into some parking lot and dragged me from the car; yelling how much of a lazy piece of shit I was and that he was taking me into the town courthouse to divorce my lazy ass.

June 1994-Petoskey, MI.

We had just come back from visiting my grandparents and I had filled my grandma in on the fact that I had taken a pregnancy test and it came back positive. My ex started yelling at me, for God knows what reason, in the living room of our apartment. The next thing I remember is him picking me up by the throat and throwing me down on the living room floor. He then proceeded to kick me repeatedly in the stomach until I was unable to breathe. He left me there on the floor; curled up in a ball, crying, and gasping for air. If the pregnancy test wasn't a false positive, I have no doubt that I lost the baby that day. My periods are always incredibly heavy with huge clots, and so I probably miscarried, with it being taken care of during my menstrual cycle. One of the worst things about that day is that I will never know for sure.

Mid-November 1994 through early Spring 1996-Fort Walton Beach, Florida.

This period of time was incredibly volatile. We were living with his parents and looking for work. I did not have a driver's license, due to a history of seizures, and had to walk to work. My ex didn't really care how difficult it was for me to walk to work as long as I brought in a pay check. I first took a job working at an after school program, that was over a two and a half mile round trip, and had to quit because I was told I was not making enough money. It was while working there that I found out I was pregnant with our first child. I then found another job working at a nursing home that wasn't as far of a walk for me. My shift was from 2:30 PM to 11:00 PM and I often found myself having to walk home at night, after my shift, and even in the rain. I was

SURVIVING DOMESTIC VIOLENCE

unable to work there for long, due to my pregnancy, and that caused a lot of problems. It was made clear to me that I had better get off my ass and find yet another job. I was very pregnant at this time, but found a job at a video store. Surprisingly, my ex managed to drive me to work. I was unable to keep that job for long, due to my pregnancy, but was told by my ex it was because I was too stupid to even hold a job at a video store. During the times I was looking for employment, he constantly reminded me that I was a lazy piece of shit, that I was stupid, that I couldn't hold down a job... Even though I was carrying his child, he found it necessary to shove me around, push me up against the nearest wall, and scream in my face. After giving birth, he refused to help me with our son. I was left to make all the formula, wash all the bottles, change all the diapers, and give all the baths. I was the one up with our boy during the nights; not him, but still I was a lazy worthless piece of shit who couldn't hold down a job.

May 1996-Fort Walton Beach, FL.

Using our rapid refund; we were moving to Niceville Fl. I had given birth to our first child on December 8th of the previous year. My ex started yelling at me that I wasn't moving our stuff into the truck fast enough, that I wasn't packing boxes fast enough, that I was a lazy piece of shit, and that I couldn't lift anything; therefore was useless to him. He then proceeded to shove me around with the furniture we were carrying; knocking me off balance with our couch. While in the moving van my ex continued with the pushing and shoving and yelling. I just remember thinking he was so darn loud in the back of the moving truck with his voice echoing off the walls like it was. I was frightened for our son and was worried he would take his anger out on our boy. As lame as it may sound, I was thankful my ex took his anger out on me only that day. I was pushed against boxes, furniture, and anything else in the back of the truck. There was very little space, so getting away was not an option for me. When he wasn't man- handling me, he took the time to yell at me for being useless and lazy.

July 1996-Niceville, FL.

I was about two and a half months pregnant with our second child. I wasn't feeling up to going out, but it was the Fourth of July and we were meeting his family to watch the fireworks at the water's edge. He yelled at me for not feeling well and how, like it or not, we were going to be with his family. He also told me I had better lose the attitude I had before we met up with his family or else. We kept arguing because I told him to go without me. He then picked me up by my throat and threw me down on to our couch. While there, he pinned me down with his body, screamed in my face, and slapped at my arms and head. When he finally got off of me, my ex just reminded me that I had better change my attitude before we met up with his family or I would end up regretting it.

Summer 1996 through February 1997-Niceville, FL.

These months were filled with arguments of me being lazy, a worthless piece of shit, a fat ass, how he had to work double shifts, and all I did was stay home and take care of our son. Mind you, I worked up until October of '96 until I was too pregnant to work as a CNA. I had even stopped working at the nursing home he was working at in order to obtain employment at a nursing home that paid more money. Before starting the new job, rumors were flying throughout the facility that my ex was having affairs or flirting with gals that worked with us. I was accused of being jealous and that I was pathetic if I honestly thought he was messing around with the women he worked with. These months were also filled with my ex constantly ridiculing me about my appearance; that he couldn't take me anywhere without me having baby puke or whatever else all over me. My friend was staying with us at the time and she took me to my OBGYN appointments and ultrasounds on her days off; my ex couldn't be inconvenienced. My ex still wasn't stepping up to the plate to help take care of our son unless it was to make himself look good in public or should I say, "look good in front of his co-workers".

Third Week of February 1997-Niceville, FL.

We got into an argument while taking our two children to my baby girl's two week check up. He was again telling me how lazy I was and what a worthless piece of shit I was that couldn't keep a job. He was mad because he worked all the time and all I did was stay home with our two children. I reminded him that he never lifted a finger to help take care of the children; no helping with baths; no helping with feeding them; no help during the middle of the night. I reminded him that he got all the sleep and I never slept between two babies and keeping up with housework. He yelled in my face; pushing my head into the car window. I got out and went behind my seat to get our daughter from the car seat. My ex turned around in his seat, yelled at me; calling me a bitch, and then punched me across the right side of my face. Our children started crying and I took off my wedding band and engagement ring and threw them at him telling him not to call me a bitch in front of our children. The wedding band went to his feet and the engagement ring bounced out of the car and into the parking lot. I walked away and tried to leave. He followed me with his car shouting out the windows that I was fucking stupid; that I was a fucking bitch; that I had better get my fucking ass in the car. After getting back into the car, he resumed shouting his usual at me. He was livid at the fact we could not find the "precious engagement ring" that he spent all that money on. I had to endure him ridiculing me under his breath the entire time while we were in the waiting room. On the way back to the apartment, my ex did nothing but yell at me for being the worthless piece of shit, the stupid one, the lazy one, and now the one that lost the engagement ring. He didn't let me live that one down for quite some time after that. It was then that

I knew whole-heartedly that money and possessions meant more to him than any human being.

March 1997 through April 1998-San Antonio, TX.

In March of 1997 we had to move from Florida to Texas, this of course was my fault. We ended up moving in with his parents during this span of time. We both got jobs working at the same assisted living home. Even though I was caring for both of our children, taking care of my responsibilities in the house, being treated like I was his mother's servant, and working any shift I could for extra money, I was still considered a lazy fat ass to my ex-husband. Living under the same roof as his mother was very difficult and I was constantly yelled at. I needed to keep my fucking mouth shut about his family, I was fucking stupid and knew nothing, that I was a worthless piece of shit. By March of '98, my ex was promoted at our place of employment. This meant I was not going to be permitted to continue working there and had to find another job. Even though his promotion was the reason I had to find another job, my ex found a way to turn it around and blame me for not finding a job quick enough and the reason we had no money.

May 1998 through October 1999-San Antonio, TX.

We finally moved out of his parents' house and into an apartment. I found another job at another assisted living home despite the fact my right eye had already gone blind. Even though I was left with the responsibilities of working at my place of employment, caring for two children, and setting up the apartment after my shift; my ex still found it necessary to continue with the name calling. I was a lazy ass, a worthless piece of shit, and I wasn't bringing in enough money. By this time rumors were flying around about my ex flirting with his employees and he was gone often; blaming it on work. The arguments were still going on about him not wanting to get me to and from work, that I wasn't making enough money, etc. I would mention the rumors of his infidelity and that only resulted in physical violence and him telling me I was stupid, jealous, and he wanted a divorce. By the spring of '99 we moved yet again into another apartment. I found a job as a domestic sales ticket agent with a popular airline. My left eye was slowly losing its sight, but I managed to still work without anyone knowing. My ex was somewhat happy that I was earning more money per hour, but angry that I wasn't working forty plus hours a week. I was, yet again, left to take care of everything at our apartment, our two children, and work until 11 o'clock at night. None of this was good enough for my ex. I was still the lazy fat ass; the worthless piece of shit… Things only got worse when I found out I had to resign from the airline in order to apply for SSDI. Because of this, my ex decided it was all my fault that we had to move back in with his parents and that I didn't have a job.

December 8th, 1999-San Antonio, TX.

We had been living back with his parents for about two months at this point and the usual arguments were going on regularly. I was, yet again, called the lazy fat ass, the worthless piece of shit, the reason we were living with his parents. I was told weekly to keep my fucking mouth shut about his family, that I was fucking stupid, etc. He was angry because I wasn't getting my SSDI fast enough, which ended up being my fault even though I had no control over that. It was our oldest child's birthday and we were fighting over the usual crap. Since I was pregnant with our third child, and my ex had a history of physical violence while I was pregnant, I ran away upstairs to our bedroom. I shut the door behind me and laid on the bed, facing the wall. The next thing I knew he had burst into the bedroom and was still yelling at me for how fucking stupid and lazy I was. I just kept facing the wall until he got up on the bed and punched me on the right side of my head. He came back into the bedroom later to tell me to get off my ass and change my attitude because it was our son's birthday and his parents would be home soon.

December 1999 through April 2000-San Antonio, TX.

These months were filled with him constantly yelling at me for being a lazy fat ass, a worthless piece of shit, etc. By this time a friend of mine worked for my ex-husband and she was telling me via phone how my ex was flirting with a certain employee at work and having an affair. When I confronted my ex-husband about the allegations, he went to his boss and had my friend fired. I was also being told, yet again, that I was stupid and jealous for absolutely no reason. He was gone a lot and still was not stepping up to the plate to help me care for our two children. By mid-April I had given birth to our third child, a boy. Even though I was blind, my ex would not help in any way, but yelled at me if I didn't do certain things to his liking. He made me feel that my blindness was my fault and that he wanted nothing to do with a woman who was, in his eyes, helpless to bring in a pay check.

Summer 2000-San Antonio, TX.

I had just gotten our youngest child off to sleep in his swing upstairs and had come down to the kitchen to get our oldest two set up at the table for dinner. I can't really remember what my ex was yelling at me for at that moment. I only remember him being all up in my face while I was trying to feed our children. I had just sat them down to fish sticks, mac and cheese, and corn and the next thing I know my ex had grabbed me around the neck; slamming me against the back door and throwing me on to the floor. While I was pinned to the floor by my ex, he proceeded to rip handfuls of hair out of my head. I moved enough across the floor to find a hard plastic dog food dish. I took the dish, slid it across the floor, and hit my ex in the ankle. He backed off for a moment, but soon resumed punching me all over and ripping more of my hair out. I could hear both of our children screaming and crying at what they saw, but I couldn't get to them. I finally got away from my ex and made it upstairs, where I locked myself in a bathroom. I am not sure how much time went by while I was in the bathroom. I just remembered I couldn't stop crying as I slowly pulled all the loose hair from my head and filled the trash can with it. The more I brushed my hair; the more hair fell out. By the time I was done, the back of my head and to the left side had several bald patches. The top of my hair was long enough to cover the damage of what he did, but I knew it was there. It took awhile for my hair to grow back in. Every time I went to brush my hair I think I cried, or at least it seemed like it... After all of that my ex blamed me for weeks about how I hurt his ankle with the dog dish; never mind the bald patches he left in my hair.

July 2000 through February 2002-San Antonio, TX.

By this time my ex was yelling at me right in front of the children. We had moved out of his parents' home by early 2001 and were working on purchasing a home. I had finally been approved for SSDI and was trying to figure out how to earn extra money to help out. These months were filled with verbal abuse; yelling in my face; pinning me against the wall with his body as he yelled at me. I was still getting no help when it came to the care of the children. Since I was totally blind my ex would make me feel I was worthless because I couldn't drive to the store to buy groceries and he was always having to do it. I was made to feel ashamed of my blindness while in public; constantly being ridiculed in stores or restaurants because my ex had to help guide me or cut up my food. His day in and day out comments of how I was so pathetic made it unbearable to be seen in public or be around any of his co-workers. He was so embarrassed by me that he tried forcing our oldest son to guide me, by holding my hand, through stores and parking lots and other public places. My ex made it way too humiliating of an experience for me to want to be in public with him, yet I had to do it and put up with him verbally bashing me under his breath. At this point the rumors had gotten back to me about my ex portraying himself as the hard working husband with the helpless and handicapped wife who couldn't lift a finger to help him take care of the children or house. It was also during these months that he began his verbal sexual abuse of me; wanting me to seduce his receptionist. I was also yelled at because he felt I couldn't keep the house clean enough or the kids clean enough or hang up his clothes the right way after doing laundry. He was also constantly yelling at me for standing up for the rights of his biological father. To him, his biological father was none of my business and his mother was never to know that he had any kind of contact with our children.

March 2002 through September 2004-San Antonio, TX.

These months were just an intensified version of the previous months/years. We moved into the new house and were pretty much the only people living on the block. This meant there was no one around to hear his fits of anger. He began yelling at our oldest son while in the backyard; calling him fucking stupid or a fucking idiot. Whenever I tried standing up to my ex; telling him not to call our son names; I was told to mind my own fucking business and that our oldest son was "his son". My ex became obsessed with the appearance of the outside and inside of our new house. It was like he had to make sure anyone who saw the house had better be jealous, envious, or highly impressed by what they saw when they came to the place. My ex had me decorate the inside of our home, but would take credit for it when his co workers/friends came over for a BBQ. I was yelled at if I didn't water his lawn enough. I was yelled at if I watered his lawn too much. I had to get up before sunrise to water his flowers in the front yard, or do it at night once the sun had set. I was yelled at if he spilled his own drink. I was yelled at if I didn't clean up the spill good enough. The kids were yelled at if they touched "his stuff". The kids were yelled at if they accidentally spilled something on "his floor" or "his table". If either myself or one of the kids did anything, shy of breathing, around "his stuff" then he would yell.

He was lying so much at this point about his severely handicapped wife, that the get-togethers he had me throw to impress our neighbors or his employees were nightmares for me. I had to do much of the work and then sit quietly as he took credit for all of it. If I tried to speak up he would tell me to shut the fuck up. It was around this time he got hooked on liquor. I knew he was hooked on it when he found out that I had mixed myself a drink using his bourbon. He yelled at me for drinking all of his liquor. I told him I had only mixed one drink and to fix the problem I would buy him a whole new bottle. As soon as I could I had a neighbor take me to the liquor store, so I could buy his bourbon; didn't matter. I was able to relax a bit during these get-togethers once he was too drunk to care. His obsession with trying to be the "Best on the Block" resulted in him purchasing a lot of things for the house that I am sure we could not afford, but again I had to keep my fucking mouth shut. I was cleaning up to three times a day, but still the inside of the house looked like "we lived in the fucking projects". When my response was that he never should have gotten married, or had children, or brought in dogs, he'd just become angry and violent. I was still the worthless piece of shit; the lazy ass; the unsupportive wife. He just had to have a dog, a large one, and I was soon cleaning up his backyard, of dog shit, on my hands and knees with two grocery bags. During this time period, he brought in four dogs; two not working out, two he kept. I was left with the job of house breaking each dog and making sure they were fed and bathed. My ex was pushing me more and more to bring strange women home, so he could catch us having sex. He was still on the fringe of an affair with his employee and soon that came to fruition. It was also during this time period that he decided the kids were better seen and not heard. He would not help me take care of any of the children, he only opened his mouth to them if it meant yelling, and he never spent any quality time with them. My ex had his own life and didn't care what happened with his family unless he was pissed about something. In an attempt to look good, he tried being a scout leader for our oldest son's troop, but that didn't last long. He also began coaching baseball, but would constantly ridicule our oldest son's inability to play baseball to his standards. I was in a car accident in February of 2004 and this resulted in three herniated discs; two in my neck, one in my very lower back. I had to endure at home physical therapy, wear a unit that pulsed electricity through my back and neck, and still take care of everything having to do with the house and kids and dogs. I was on pain medication that did no good and was supposed to lift nothing over ten pounds. Even with restrictions being placed upon me, my ex cared less about any of it. It just only made me lazier in his eyes and more of a worthless piece of shit. I was supposed to do everything inside and outside the house plus take care of the children plus care for his dogs with three herniated discs, oh and in full make up and dressy clothing. When I tried to explain I could not do everything around the house in a skirt and high heels AND in full make up, he would just say gals at his work did it and would compare me to a cow.

September 2004-San Antonio, TX.

While my brother and nephew were visiting from New Hampshire, my ex- husband cornered me in our bedroom and began an argument. He was yelling at me for having a good relationship with my brother and why didn't I treat him as well as I treated my brother. I had told him my brother didn't make me feel like a worthless piece of shit and a whore. I also reminded him that it wasn't my brother I was married to or he who was sticking his dick into his employee. After saying that, my ex threw me into our bedroom closet and ripped my silver chain off my neck. He then pulled me from the closet and pushed me towards the bed asking if I wanted to be treated like a whore because that is exactly how he could treat me. He began slapping my upper body and head. I finally stood up for myself and slapped him back, in the face. He didn't like that and grabbed me by my upper right arm; throwing me to the bed. While there, he kept choking me and spitting in my face saying how much he hated me; that I was a bitch; a lazy piece of shit; and how dare I slap him. He left an enormous bruise on the underside of my right arm that was instantly visible to my family and his. Since he could not have me talking about it honestly, I had to lie to anyone who saw it; saying I hit it on a door knob while trying to kneel to the floor.

October 2004 through May 2005-San Antonio, TX.

During these months, my ex openly had an affair with one of his employees. The lying, verbal abuse, and physical abuse only got worse. By the end of October 2004 my ex moved out of the house. He didn't feel it necessary to let me, or his own children, know where he was going or how to contact him. As soon as I could, I took my SSDI out of his bank account and started my own account with it. I knew I had to bring in more money to the house to support our three children, so I began making holiday center pieces and wreaths to sell at our children's school. I also had a friend who encouraged me to sell beauty products. This brought in the extra money I needed. I also put our two oldest children on the free lunch program at school. When my ex found out, he yelled at me about making our children look like welfare kids. I went to our children's school and signed up our kids to see the school counselor; letting them know the circumstances at the house. This further enraged my ex because I spoke out about the situation; making him "look bad". I was only thinking of our children and he was only thinking about his reputation in the community. I had no idea where he was or what to tell the children. He had flaunted his affair in front of our children;

bringing her into our home; taking her with him while with our kids. The children felt their father was choosing his girlfriend over them and I had no idea what to say. Since 2001 I had a cell phone contract in my name. My ex racked up the cell phone bill so much that I could not keep up with paying the bill. I had to cancel the contract on each phone, which pissed off my ex and started him yelling. I tried to explain I needed the money to go towards our children and not his cell phone bill. On my own, I decorated the house for Halloween, Thanksgiving, and Christmas for our kids. I was desperately trying to keep some normalcy for the kids while their father only paid attention to himself and his affair. I took what money I had; from my SSDI, selling the crafts I made and beauty products; and purchased a majority of the children's Christmas gifts on my own. It took me a full week, due to my herniated discs, to get the Christmas tree up and decorated, but I managed it. My ex came to the house to see the kids and noticed all that I had accomplished and lied his way back into the house. He instantly started in with his verbal abuse, in private and public, and once Christmas was over with; moved out again. Again, I have no idea where he went. After a few weeks he lied his way back into living with us. He was still having an affair; which he was now openly flaunting in the neighborhood by bragging about how much his employee "was in love with him"; and was making plans to leave for a new job in Florida. While he was in Florida, settling things for his new job, he met up with his next affair. His abuse of me got worse. While he was in Florida, he yelled at me via phone about being a worthless piece of shit, being lazy, and that I was the one having an affair. When he was back in Texas it was more of the same, just face to face. I finally had enough and told him to leave for good and go be with the employee he was having the affair with. I let him know that not only would I make sure he supported his children, but that his girlfriend would make

SURVIVING DOMESTIC VIOLENCE

sure he supported her, her daughter, and her grandchild. This caused another fight, got him to lie about wanting to make the marriage work, and convince me to allow him to move all of us to Florida in order to "start a new life and get away from all the rumors".

April 2005-Boynton Beach, FL.

While on a trip to Florida, that my ex convinced me was to renew our marriage and start a new life, all hell broke loose. He kept me basically locked up in some hotel room while he checked out his new job and whatever else he did to stay away from me. I was brought out of the hotel room once to see where he would be working and once to go to dinner. While at his soon to be place of employment, he left me alone, sitting in a chair, so he could walked the property by himself. While at dinner, he humiliated me under his breath; telling me I was worthless, an embarrassment to him, etc. Since I could not endure that with a smile, the abuse got worse once we left the restaurant. On the flight back to Texas, he yelled at me under his breath about how great his mistress was and how worthless I was. He told me that he was done with me and our marriage was over once we were back in San Antonio. When we got off the plane, he made me try to follow him without help from a sight guide or my cane. No one could have known I was completely blind and I had to struggle with my suitcase while trying to hear where he was walking. This went on throughout the airport and parking area. I finally made it to his vehicle and entered it to only hear fits of his rage. I was nothing but an embarrassment to him, a worthless piece of shit, a lazy fat ass. I was bringing him down and wasn't good enough for him. I reminded him again to just leave and be with his employee, that only wanted him for money he didn't have, and to leave me and the children alone. He wasn't living at the house anymore, and by the looks of it, juggling two affairs.

End of May 2005 through End of July 2005-San Antonio, TX.

By the end of May my ex had moved to Florida; leaving me to sell our house in Texas. I was responsible for maintaining everything inside and outside the house, the children, and the real estate office. I still had to deal with the herniated discs, so certain things like taking care of his dogs, the pool, and the yard was difficult. My ex flew back to Texas long enough to ridicule me for how I was keeping things around the house. He barked orders at me, yelled to the point that now the neighbors heard, and went back to Florida. By the first week of July my ex made me allow our oldest son to go out to Florida to be with him; giving him control over me. Come mid-July I had to move myself, our two youngest children, and his two dogs in with his parents. This was a nightmare. I felt like a prisoner in their home; only coming out of the room to feed the children or take the dogs to go to the bathroom. I was only yelled at via phone if I mentioned how bad it was staying with his parents. I was still dealing with selling the house, trying to find a way to get his dogs to Florida, and make sure me and the kids weren't yelled at by my ex mother-in-law. At the end of July, I flew with our two youngest children to be with their father and our oldest son in Florida. We had to spend a few nights in one of the rooms my ex's assisted living home had vacant. I was not allowed out of the room because no one was supposed to know my ex was married. (Hind sight is 20/20; can't let his mistress find out) He would take the kids out of the room for a few minutes, if they got to rowdy, but left me behind.

August 1, 2005 through September 15, 2005-Lake Worth, FL. We moved into an apartment where I was left to set up the place on my own and get it to where it was livable. My ex spent most of his time who knows where and I was forced to find my own way, with our three children, to the school they would be attending and get all three registered. It was so hot that day and we got lost. I had no one to call and no cell phone to use if I did have anyone to call. The kids and I were finally picked up by a woman who took us to the school. I had the kids rest while I gathered all the necessary paper work. I then had to encourage the children to walk all the way back to the apartment with me. I managed to get the apartment all set up and the children registered for school and set up appointments with a doctor for their physicals. When my ex was at the apartment all he did was verbally abuse me in front of the children. By now he was yelling even more at our children and began to abuse the two dogs. The dogs were such a nervous wreck that they were vomiting and relieving themselves where they stood when my ex began yelling. By September 15 I was on a plane to San Antonio, TX to have my neck surgery. My ex was pissed off that I was going, but knew once the surgery was done I was getting a settlement.

Mid-September 2005 through October 1, 2005-San Antonio, TX. While back in Texas to have my neck surgery and recuperate, my ex would constantly call me and either verbally abuse me; saying never to come back to Florida; or attempt to get phone sex out of me. I was staying with one of my best gal pals at the time and she heard pretty much all of it. Since I knew I was going to be on massive restrictions for a few months, I had the doctor write out everything I was not allowed to do. I unloaded to my surgeon about the abusive ways of my ex, and what he would force me to do, so the doctor wrote up two pages of things I would not be able to do and for how long. The doctor told me to post them on our fridge to remind my ex that I was not supposed to do much of anything. My ex did everything he could to humiliate me over the phone, but I was not about to leave our children alone with him in Florida.

October 1, 2005-San Antonio, TX.

I received a phone call telling me I had no choice but to come back to Florida so he could fly to New Jersey for his nephew's baptism/christening that weekend. He knew I was on massive restrictions and in a hard C-collar. I wasn't even cleared by the doctor to fly anywhere, but my ex didn't care. I didn't have the money to change my plane ticket because I had to pay for all of my medications. My ex didn't care about this either and just kept up the verbal abuse over the phone; telling me to get my fucking ass back to Florida and he didn't care what I had to do to get there. I borrowed the money from the friends I was staying with and flew back to Florida. Since I had not been fully cleared by the doctor to fly, he gave me a list of things to do in order to make it easier on my neck. I had to lie down whenever possible and had to hold my neck during take offs and landings. I just remember being tired, in pain, and so drugged up.

October 2005-Lake Worth, FL.

When I came home I placed the list of restrictions that were to be followed for the next eight to twelve weeks on our refrigerator. I had the surgeon write them up because he knew how my ex-husband was and I was hoping my ex would read them and actually care about my health and not expect me to do everything around the apartment. When he came back from his get-a-way, he removed my list of restrictions and shoved them in a drawer. I was told "here is a quarter; call someone that actually gives a shit". He constantly yelled that I was lazy, a worthless piece of shit, that I was a bitch. I was made to go against all of my restrictions. I was made to pick up the golden retriever, place him in the tub, and bathe him. I was verbally abused until I would get on my hands and knees to scrub the floors of the apartment and clean the rest of the apartment; including both restrooms. I was forced to take the dog out to the restroom; walking him around the entire pond; while my ex sat around and watched TV. He was gone quite a bit to be with his mistress during this time. Again I was left to care for the kids and walk to the grocery store (over one mile one way) with them, my cane, and a hard C-collar on. My ex left me with no money for groceries. When I mentioned that to him, and the fact I was having to walk with the kids as far as I was, he just told me to "Do whatever you have to fucking do to get the children food". I was forced to have sex even though I wasn't supposed to have sex for at least eight weeks. I was told I was still his wife and he could do whatever he wanted to. We were hit with a hurricane, towards the end of October, and instead of him helping me shut our hurricane shutters and prepare; he sat in his bedroom watching TV. I eventually had the people that worked for the apartment complex help me prepare for the storm. It was humiliating to have to admit to the folks running the apartment complex that my husband was in the next room, watching his TV, and refusing to help me. Just before the hurricane hit, my ex found an excuse to leave me and our children alone in the apartment. I had made friends with a lady a couple halls away though and went to help her with her shutters and get her, along with her daughter, down to our apartment. During the hurricane and after, my ex spent 99% of his time at work and with his mistress. He forced me and our children from our apartment and up to his brothers. This was so his mistress would have a place to live. When we returned to the apartment it wreaked of his mistress' cigarette smoke and my ex lied; saying his employees stopped in for showers because they had no place else to go. Without the help of the children's father, I purchased the children Halloween costumes and candy buckets. Since the hurricane basically trashed everything, and many folks weren't passing out candy, I went with my friend and the kids to trick or treat at a local mall. My ex-husband was full of lies and verbal abuse during this time. When he finally showed up at the apartment he went off on me about the lack of candy the kids got from trick or treating. When I yelled back that at least I was with our children and attempted to celebrate Halloween with them, he just went into a fit of rage. There were constant threats of him breaking my neck. With my neck in a C-collar and not even close to being healed; I was scared that he would either kill me or paralyze me if I didn't do what he wanted.

November 2005-Lake Worth, FL.

While still recovering from neck surgery, and in my hard C-collar, I was constantly being verbally abused and my ex-husband started in with the physical abuse again. He was openly yelling at me in front of the children, and once they were out of the room, he would push me and shove me around. He was grabbing me and threatening to snap my neck, break my neck, and choke me. He was calling me a bitch in front of our daughter and I told him not to call me names in front of the children. The times he wasn't at the apartment, he was spending his time with his mistress. On our 12th wedding anniversary, November 13th, he shouted at me to get the fuck out of the apartment; that if I didn't leave he would break my neck; that I never should have come back from Texas after my surgery. After yelling at me to get out he went to be with his mistress and I called my brother for help; that was on a Sunday. By Friday morning at 7am, I was in a taxi headed for the airport. By the following Sunday, his mistress was moved in to the apartment. Since my ex knew my settlement from the car accident had come through, he forced me to pay off an IRS bill of $1800 and purchase two weeks of groceries for himself and our children before I left. He also threatened me into cleaning the entire apartment, wash all the clothes, and deal with the remaining dog during the few days I had left before my flight. I was allowed to only leave with a suitcase that had some clothes and shoes in it and another suitcase with a few personal items he let me keep.

I obviously didn't go into detail when I wrote my little journal of abuse and I didn't write about the crud I had to endure after being kicked out in November of 2005. The main point of the exercise was to get out on the page the major things I needed to purge my soul of. It was a good thing for me to do, but after reading what I had gone through, I was ashamed... I was ashamed that I allowed another human being to have that much control over me. I was ashamed that I allowed the father of my children to verbally and emotionally abuse them. I was ashamed that I allowed my supposed husband to treat me so cruelly in front of our children. Where the hell was my spine during all those years of abuse? My abuser beat me into a shell of a person and by the middle of November 2005, I thought I would never recover from any of it. Leaving my children that Friday felt like my heart was ripped out. I don't remember much of the plane ride up to see my big brother... I just remember so much pain. What gives any man the right to do this to a woman? I just don't understand it and probably never will. I need a cup of coffee. It is my excuse to get away from this damn computer and shake off the sadness of that Friday morning in November...

I'm back. Does anyone even remember where we left off before I tossed in the history of my abuse? We were on the obstacle of the in-laws; oh joy of joys... I had already covered the Blackmailing in-law and was about to discuss the Spy in-law. I was angry that day though and decided it best not to go any further with that topic. No excuses now and we need to press on.

Unfortunately, as I may have stated before, I had the Spy in-laws. Okay, the Spy mother-in-law and her husband who stands by her no matter what horrible decision she makes. (I am not blaming the man; just stating a fact) Man, how do I go about this without it reading like a personal attack against my ex-in-laws? I know what I want to say, but I don't want to paint a portrait of an evil woman who allowed her son to beat down his wife; the mother of her grandchildren. Granted, that is what she is and that is what she sat back and watched happen, but I digress... Hmmm... Alright, I'll try this approach and if it takes me down the path of talking about how much I can't stand my ex's mother, I'll stop.

In order to be in the proper frame of mind when reading about the Spy in-law, think of the whole situation as if it were a cold war and your in-laws are the double agents. They show a false loyalty to their homeland (their son), but then behave like the enemy country (you) has that same loyalty. In all actuality they are out for themselves and will lean towards whomever they feel will give them the most benefits in the end.

What do I mean by benefits? To be brutally honest; who will let them see or have other forms of contact with their future grandchildren. Geez, I am already getting mad just thinking about what I will have to write; darn it... I am sure a lot of you are thinking, "But we don't have any children yet."; doesn't matter. You may not have children right off the bat, but they look at you as the Potential Mother of their grandchildren. This means the charm is turned on and the spying starts immediately. I will reiterate again that I AM NOT TALKING ABOUT MY EX STEP-FATHER-IN- LAW. I believe he has blinders on to anything his wife does, but deep down has a kind heart.

So, back to the whole charm/spy mentality of these people. This is how it works... They portray themselves to be the kind of in-law that thinks you are the best gal for their son, that you are incredible, and that the soon-to-be marriage is a match made in heaven. At least this is how they are to your face. The moment your back is turned they are telling others in their family that you are wretched, lazy, a bitch, or whatever else they can make up about you. Sadly, this type of in-law represents pretty much the rest of that side of the family and gossip is king! Their charming ways are so slick that you will begin to confide in them about your own dysfunctional family or little problems you are having with their son. Oh yeah, they are hanging on your every word; not. They listen to what they consider nothing short of you whining, so they can keep a firm grasp on what is going on behind the scenes. The Spy in-law is already keeping track of who will give them what they ultimately want. So, they begin to play the fence in hopes that your marriage to their son is so screwed up that you will not confide in him about the ugliness they spread. In essence, they pit you and your husband against one another and that is how they play the game.

How does the game start? The spy listens to the fits of rage by their son and then waits for you to come crying to them. If you don't come crying to them, they will hint they heard an argument and let you know if you need anything that they are "there for you". Now, if you are stupid enough to fall for their lies, then they will take what you said, twist it, and tell their son. This will go back and forth, like a tennis match, until the D-bomb drops. Once a divorce is in place the Spy in-law will make a B line to which ever one has their grandchildren. These in-laws are slicker than shit though and try to maintain some sort of fake civility with the parent without the grandchildren in case the tides change. Man, I am disgusted… My first husband's mother is a horrible person! I do not say she is a horrible person without due cause. She played the game as best she could, and still does. I am sorry, but I knew you were two-faced when I was married to your son, I know you lie to my children about me, I know all too well how you lie to the kids about anyone you feel is a threat to you, and you taught this lovely way of treating people to your son! You spawned an abuser, you fed the abuser all the hate and rage necessary, and then you let him loose. You did such a good job messing with his head that he'll even turn on you half of the time if you don't give him what he wants. How does that make you feel, hmmm? Are you proud of the beast you raised? I warned all of those reading this that there was a good chance I would go off about my ex's mother; how could I not? I'll move on though and I truly hope I did a fair enough job explaining what the Spy in-law is like.

I am very sorry ladies, but I won't be doing any writing this morning. I was roused this morning, by my husband's alarm clock, from a horrible nightmare I am unable to shake off. I am thankful that I do not remember much of it, but remembering the gist has me wanting to either curl up and die or take an endless crazy hot shower. Even though my ex had gastric bypass surgery, I still see him as a 400 pound predator. In my nightmare he was topping 500 pounds and naked. He had forced me into a warehouse where old furniture was stored. He ripped my clothes off and was about to rape me. I just remember screaming at him that I was married and that if he touched me in any way that my husband would feel I cheated on him. I just kept begging him not to touch me. He tied me up to a broken post from one of those four poster beds and left me there. I watched him walk back and forth; carrying things towards the bed that he was going to use on me for his own sexual enjoyment... This is why I cannot write this morning. I need to fill my head of thoughts that are far removed from my ex-abuser and/or his family members. I thought unloading it to my husband this morning would help; it didn't. When I hugged my husband good-bye (he had work) I just broke down crying in his arms. I love my husband, adore him, but to even have another man touch me in a nightmare feels wrong and dirty to me. I hate my first husband right now for all he put me through and all the nightmares he left me with. The fucking nightmares that feel so real that you can't shake them for hours and hours... So, I am going to wipe the tears from my face, blow my nose, and hopefully get lost in a book by one of my most favorite of writers. Maybe tomorrow will be a better day for me.

One where I can feel like I am writing from a distance about abuse, instead of like I am still living it. Raw emotion is good when you are writing; just not this morning...

Well ladies, I am back for another round. I have recovered from yesterday and the demons that shook me are no more. When my husband came home from work I told him how I spent my morning crying and got no writing done. Just so you know... My husband has not read one stitch of what I have written on these pages. He can't stand knowing the fact my first husband abused me for so long; let alone stomach the crud I am dealing with when it comes to my children. I can't imagine how he'd feel if he knew everything. It is not that I am keeping things from him out of shame or anything like that. It is just that my husband is a gentle-hearted man and I know he would take on any pain of mine if he could. I suppose all of this nonsense chatter is getting us no where this morning. I guess I just want to keep reminding you ladies, in my own strange way, that I am human and put my pants on each day like the rest of you. We all have our ups and our downs; yesterday was a down for me. I would be remiss if I did not share all of who I am with all of you reading these pages. I don't want to be a detached person writing about the past. Granted, I don't want to dredge up horrible memories, ghosts, or flashbacks in the attempts to get my point across, but I do want to remind you all I am real and what I went through was real. You are not alone during your down days; I am here with you. You are also not alone during your up days; I am here celebrating with you!

Obstacle Six: Our Family Members

I know it is difficult to fathom that while on our path to recovery and victory over domestic violence that we could have a family member weighing us down, but it happens. It happened to me. I don't think she meant to do what she did, but I'll get into my own situation later. Hold on, let me suck down the rest of this cold cup of coffee and snag a fresh one. Bet you ladies think I can't write without coffee… You are probably correct! Glad I am not being timed on how long it takes to get back in front of this computer. While down getting coffee, my taste buds screamed for a peanut butter and jelly sandwich. I am one of those gals who likes lunch stuff for breakfast and breakfast stuff for dinner; not all the time, mind you. I believe I was a tad too eager for my fresh cup of coffee though because I burned my tongue… Okay, one peanut butter and jelly sandwich down; one cup of coffee now drinkable. Let's move on…

There maybe more than two kinds of family members that present themselves as obstacles, but I can only think of two. You have the first type that is born out of that lovely group of brainwashing ladies I discussed earlier and the type that has been through an abusive relationship, has not recovered from it, and transfers all she feels on to you. To compound the problem with this second kind of family member is the fact they are more than likely older than you and feel they are right about everything and you are right about nothing. I am not trying to scare any of you away from getting support from your family members. I just highly suggest you out your situation to the right ones. Here is Suggestion #1: If you were brainwashed by any woman in your family, then DO NOT confide in them. Here is Suggestion #2: DO NOT look for unbiased support from an older sister or female cousin or aunt that you know, spot on, was or is involved in her own abusive relationship. I am totally not knocking the aforementioned group of ladies. All I am saying is you wouldn't try to recover from alcoholism with the support of a family member who drinks booze like a fish; get my meaning? Lastly, Suggestion #3: For absolutely no reason WHAT SO EVER should you run to the very parents that raised you up in a dysfunctional childhood in the first place and expect them to understand. Again, I am not knocking my parents or anyone else's. I am sure most parents did the best they could when it came to raising us. You have to look at who taught your parents just how to be parents before attacking them for not being "perfect". I am not saying, once you are on the road to recovery, that you cannot confide in these family members later on. Hell, you might even end up having a stronger relationship with them than you had before. Since I believe I did a better than average job of describing these types of family members, I think I will continue by telling you a little story of my own...

As I said earlier, I came up here from Florida to stay with my big brother. He gave me the emotional security I knew I needed, but also gave me the space to come to him when I was ready to talk. His first reaction was anger towards my ex, who he treated like a brother, for what he had done to me and, I suppose, surprise that I had never said anything about it in all those years. He never judged me or went on the attack for not speaking up and asking for help. He listened to me and loved me; pure and simple. Now, not all my family members were like this. I also have an older sister. She, herself, had an abusive marriage and train wreck of a divorce that she hadn't fully recovered from when I arrived up here. All the mistakes she felt she had made during her marriage or divorce process or just feelings in general were heaped on to me. Like I said, I am sure she didn't mean to approach the situation as she did, but... I am not one to fight over material things or money or stuff like that; you can't take it with you when you leave this earth. Not to mention that no amount of money or pretty things can mend a beaten down soul. I am also not one who feels it is right to "stick it" to someone just because they have wronged you. I believe that is what karma is for. When dealing with the divorce papers though, my "I know what is best for you" sister made her opinion very clear and on more than one occasion.

What did this cause? It only caused more grief for me. I went unknowingly to a sister for help, who in hind sight was emotionally drowning herself at the time. Her ex- husband and family, she felt, were screwing her over and all her hatred was the underlying theme to her advice for me. I was miserable as it was; I didn't want to fight, but here was my older sister demanding I fight for this and I demand that and I refuse to do this or that. I am sure, in her mind, she felt I was going to go through the same mess she had and she wasn't going to have that happen. It ended up turning into a nightmare that only pushed my sister and I further apart from one another. My sister even got to suggesting that she "knew I was still in love with my husband and wanted it to all work out". (I'm sorry, what? You honestly meant that when you said it?) My repeated attempts to explain to a sister, who hadn't seen me very much since she left home when I was barely thirteen, fell on deaf ears. She was older than me, she was wiser than me, she had a perfect life. Okay, that is not true, but I am sure that is what she was thinking. I truly believe she wanted to use me to fix the mistakes she felt she had made for so many years in her own life/marriage; right all of the wrongs done to her; and she shouldn't have tried to do that. Again, I am totally not knocking my sister; just saying she was misguided. Our family really does only want the best for us. The thing is, we are the only people who truly know what that is. My advice to anyone who has a family member or friend that turns to them when trying to get out of an abusive relationship... Just listen and give lots of hugs. Our minds are already reeling from the bullshit we have been put through. The last thing we need is to be told what to do! Just love us and keep your opinions to yourself, unless we ask for them.

I understand I run, yet again, the risk of offending some people by what I wrote above. Those would be the people who I described and therefore are only taking offense to the truth. Those are also probably the same people asking themselves if I keep my trap shut and opinions to myself. In response to that? Yes, I keep my opinions to myself. I learned the hard way which friends were true friends of mine and which ones played the fence (will explain later), and I don't want to be a bad friend to anyone. Just yesterday I had a girlfriend call me with some weight on her shoulders. We talked a bit and I DID have to fight the urge to give my opinion or pass judgment. Thankfully, she said she would call me back and I took that time to re-evaluate what kind of friend I wanted to be and my girlfriend needed me to be. Now, if she calls back, I know to be a good listener and sounding board for her. I love my friend and want to be there for her emotionally. I know I would only scare her off if I made her feel it wasn't safe to unload her problems to me. This confession is a great segue into the next topic I want to cover; friends...

Once we have managed to admit we are victims of domestic violence and that we are going to need help to make it through our recovery; where do we go? Our gut reaction is to run to family or friends first. As I warned above though, we have to watch which family members we run to. I didn't mention the dilemma with choosing which friends to confide in though. You would think our friends would be the safest place to run, but they aren't. We have our true friends and those who sit on the fence. Those that sit on the fence look good on the surface, but down deep they end up sabotaging our recovery. Gosh, maybe I should take the two types of friends and discuss them separately. I wouldn't say our friends are obstacles, but I would say they are like little hiccups in the road if we do not choose wisely whom to talk to.

What the heck is my deal today? It is only Wednesday, but my head is screwing with me into feeling it is Saturday or something.

I am sure that little piece of useless information means nothing to anyone reading this, but when you have a routine of writing Monday through Friday, each morning, this sort of thing tosses your controlling butt right off the truck! Alright, I was talking last Friday about friends and named the two different types. In case you are wondering, seeing this is now Wednesday, I took Monday and Tuesday to write about something else. I believe, when you are trying to wade through the swamp of abuse, there are two categories your friends fall into. Oh, it doesn't happen while you are keeping quiet about your situation. It happens as soon as you open your mouth and speak out about the abuse. Odd thing about coming to this realization is that, in your heart, you want to believe all of your friends fall into the True Friend category, but they don't. Sadly, the friends you thought were true blue may decide it is best for them to neither be true to you or your abuser. These folks sit on the fence and pretend to care about you and the beast that abused you. Before I get ahead of myself, and confuse all who are reading this, I will break the two apart and speak of them separately.

So much for me writing anymore today... Even though I work with headphones on, I can still hear a pack of little ones screaming their fool heads off outside. Don't get me wrong, I like children. I just prefer mine or the type that you know will visit and then leave. For some reason the noises and shouts from my own children sound like the singing of angels, but the same crud coming from someone else's child just annoys the heck out of me.

Outing myself to my friends was like turning on the light and watching the cockroaches scatter; one group go one way, another group another way. In your head you are imagining that all of your friends will stand by you; nope. Here is how it works... Even if you are just dealing with a divorce, you will have the folks you thought were true friends running in every direction to avoid becoming collateral damage. I only had a handful of gals I considered my friends, but even with that small group of ladies; just one riding the fence was devastating to me.

The true friend is the one who is going to pick you up off the ground and ask no questions. They will support you, yell at the top of their lungs what a scum bag your abuser is during the appropriate moments, dry your tears while they cry with you, and make you laugh when you need it most. They are the first to come to your defense, but will give you the "what for" when you become just a tad irrational. And let's face it, when coming out of the closet with the fact you are a victim of domestic violence there will be moments you are a tad off center. They are true friends; what else is there to say?

The Fence-sitters won't make themselves known right away. They will fool you into believing you have their complete confidence and that they have your back. This is a lie… I am not sure if the Fence-sitters are delusional or what. They will not help you on your journey to recovery. These type of folks will only crush you the same way your abuser did. Okay, not exactly the same way. You believe in their friendship like you believed in the "love" your abuser had for you. You believe every word they say in support of you like you believed every lie dished out at you by your abuser. These people are out for themselves like your abuser is out for themselves. Are you getting my point? Since these types of supposed friends don't show their true colors until it is crunch time; it is heart wrenching for you when the truth comes out. You put all of who you are into the jacked up relationship with your abuser only to be knocked down physically and emotionally. Then you reach out for whom you consider to be a real friend and end up getting knocked down again emotionally by them. It sucks if you find you have one of these supposed friends. To go years investing yourself only to find they aren't friends at all really sucks! Finding out you have people like this in your life is going to shake your world and all that you believed to be true. You will be angry, then sad, then not care at all, then angry again. What you go through emotionally is crazy when you find you have been betrayed, yet again, by someone you cared about.

I really did believe all my friends would choose me, but I was wrong. Looking back on all of it, I should have realized that any person you meet through your abuser, be they man or woman, will ride the fence or choose to remain friends with your abuser. I do not understand this way of thinking at all. I am disgusted today just thinking about those false friends who claim to love you and your kids, while the whole time they are still friends with your abuser. I am as disgusted with people like this as I am with those damn Spy in-laws. As you can tell by the previous sentences; I am not going to be objective about fence riding friends! I was going to separate the two types of friends and expand more on each, but I am too emotionally invested and think instead that I will write a sort of letter to each type of friend. That way I'll be able to purge my soul of all the good and bad I feel about this subject and get my point across on how to spot the true friend and the one that is not. First though I need to take something for this rockin' headache…

I am back and want to dive into my letters. I am feeling totally pumped up emotionally about each type of friend, so be prepared for the True Friend sappy letter and the I hope you sleep well at night you back stabber letter. Sarcasm abounds! Thing is, I only had one friend that I thought was a true one and turned out not to be. So, those gals who proved true will know, without a doubt, that I am writing about them. To the one who sat on the fence, deceiving me; you will know who you are… I suppose I am so wounded by this latter person because here I was, going through Hell, and she knew it. She just chose, what I feel, was the "if she doesn't know, it won't hurt our friendship" approach. I'll get into that more with her letter I suppose. And here we gooooo…

To Jules, Jen, Tammy, and Nan:

I need to start off this letter to you ladies by saying, "I love you". Since you know me as well as you all do, you know I don't throw my love around lightly. It took me, what seemed like forever, to tell all of you what was going on in my little world. When I started coming clean though, not one of you turned your back on me or doubted me or made me feel like I was making it all up. I realize domestic violence is supposed to happen to other folks and never touch our lives, but life doesn't work that way. Not only were you ladies true sisters, but your husbands proved they would step up and be my big brothers. All of you, and your children, were constant reminders to me and my three that life would be alright and in doing so, kept us going. You gals took me in and didn't allow me to wallow in self-pity. You let me cry if I needed to cry; made me laugh when I didn't think I could; raged against my abuser with me; gave me strength when I thought I had none. You and yours became my family when mine was miles upon miles away from me. I don't think I could ever thank you enough for all you have done for me. Each one of you gave me something a little different with your friendship. Jules, you are my rock. Jen, I have always felt you were like a long hug that provided love, comfort, and security. Tammy, you are my smart ass sistah that held me up, but also allowed me to hold her up when she needed it. Nan, you are a blessing; a surrogate Mom, sister, and aunt all rolled up in to one bubbly southern gal. All of you brought out the best of me when I had thought it was crushed beyond all recognition. I put myself out there by taking the risk that I did. I have never regretted taking that leap of faith with any of you. You ladies came into my life when I needed it the most and I will never be able to thank you enough or show just how much all of you mean to me. Even though we are all spread out across the map, there isn't a day that goes by that I do not think of you or about how much I love all of you. All of you are amazing women that I am proud to have met and to be able to consider you my sistahs.

And to you:

Please tell me what the heck you were thinking by what you did? I should have known the day I told you I was being abused that you were not going to believe a word I said. We sat there in your car and I poured out my heart to you and trusted you! I should have known he had already gotten to you when you replied to my plea for help with, "He has always told me that he knows better than to lay a hand on you because you would instantly call the cops". Was his lie really that easy to fall for; to believe? He was screwing his employee, your co-worker, and you knew it. Did you just figure he would stop at having an affair and not raise a hand to me? He moved out and you said nothing. He flaunted his affair and you said nothing. What kind of friend did you think you were being? I don't understand! And when all the shit hit the fan you kept me preoccupied so I wouldn't break under the weight of it all. If I had known you were also being "supportive" of the man who abused me for so long, I would have stayed away from you. What you did was not friendship or sisterhood. It was your weak way of protecting your own ass from any fucking fallout! Were you afraid he would fire you if you defended me; the woman he was BEATING? How could you play me like that and still sleep at night? Our children played together. I was there for you when things weren't so great in your life and you just played me as a show of your gratitude. Damn it, why did I put my trust in you as a friend? I truly should have known better. And all this time I felt I had treated you horribly and was continually asking you to forgive my behavior. The whole time I was trying to do right by you, you were secretly befriending my abuser. To make matters worse I knew when the divorce was going on that he would attack my character and portray me as a handicap who could not care for our children. I begged you to write a letter on my behalf and was met with nothing, but silence from you. Now I know why... All the months I heard nothing back from you and here you were keeping in touch with him via email and phone and FB; unbelievable. The least you could have done is stepped up and picked a flipping side! I need only honesty and you couldn't even give me that when I confronted you about what I found out. I loved you; thought you to be a sister; and you didn't care about anything, but yourself. God forbid you would stand up for what was right. You knew about his cheating, you knew about his abuse of me, you knew how he mentally screwed with my kids, and you didn't care because it wasn't you he was cheating on, it wasn't you he was abusing, it wasn't your children being mentally fucked up. What bothers me in all of this, other than your betrayal, is that I feel nothing for you as a human being. That fact bothers me because I have that same exact feeling for my ex-husband. It is a nothingness that screams out that you may well as not even have existed in my life. I can't even be mad at you or hate you. Feeling nothing is very sad; very sad. If you had come to me with a broken heart to admit you were being abused and that your husband was cheating on you, I would have believed you and found a way to beat your man to the ground! I wouldn't have let you cry on my shoulder and then went to your man and let him cry on my shoulder. You should have been a true friend. If you couldn't have stepped up and been a true friend to me and shown support for my situation, then you should have been up front about it. All this time you were just covering your own ass, unbelievable...

Then to add insult to injury, you didn't even fight for our friendship when I told you it would be hard to trust you with the most intimate of things going on in my life when I knew you were in contact with my ex. Your response to that? You pretty much said "oh well" and picked my abuser over me. How does it feel to know you chose a liar and a master manipulator as a friend over someone who would have died for you? I honestly didn't realize you were that weak; sad. I loved you once, I loved your family once, I had faith in you and our friendship once; not anymore.

The reason I am so insanely passionate about the topic of friendship among women is because you can never look at men the same way after you have been a victim of domestic violence. It takes a lot out of you when you finally decide to open up to your friends. It is like you are literally walking off a cliff and are hoping your friends will catch you before you hit the ground and die. My true gal pals caught me long before I reached the ground and that is what makes all the difference. If you have a friend (supposed friend) that is riding the fence during your recovery phase; kick their asses to the curb, put them out with the trash, think no more of them. If you have taken that leap off the cliff, you will need all of your strength to get better; to begin living. Those folks that sit on the fence only suck out your soul and leave you as empty as your abuser did. I am not saying any of this out of anger for the woman who said she was my friend. I am saying this because it is the truth and I don't want other women to go through unnecessary pain while they are trying to get back on their feet.

I understand that a lot of what I write may sound nasty or cruel or whatever, but it isn't. I am only telling it like it is. When I started writing all of what I went through, each word I typed was full of rage and hatred and wishes of a long drawn out death to anyone who wronged me. Now? Well, now I only have pity for those who wrong other people, deliberately hurt other people, who lie and deceive, and who do not care about the well-being of others. If you happen to be one of the aforementioned people; deal with it... Not everyone who picks up this book and peruses it will be happy about what they read. I don't care. I am not writing this book for them. I am writing this book for anyone who has been knocked down, dragged through the mud, and mentally toyed with just because another person can't control their anger. Violence, of any kind, is flipping wrong and someone needs to say something! You are not alone! I am no longer alone since I have decided to put my life in print! Stand up ladies; be heard. God knows I realize how scary it is to let it out that you are a victim of violence, but we have to do it. If we don't speak out; they win… Do you want them to win? Do you want the cycle of abuse to just keep going as if nothing is wrong with the picture it paints about us as individuals and as a society?

Yes, I understand I went off on a little tangent; I am not sorry. I can't stress enough the importance of speaking out against your abuser; not just for yourself, but for others you might be able to help or encourage. There is a story, and I don't know all the facts, about a lady who had no children and wanted to leave her abuser. She made her plans to go and was just about ready to make her move towards freedom. Her abuser got wind of her plans, but said nothing. The next morning she awoke, went down to the kitchen, and found a newspaper clipping on the table. It was a story about a man who beat, and killed, the wife who was trying to leave him. The abusive husband saw his wife reading the article he left out for her, walked up to her, pointed at the article, and said, "That could be you if you don't watch it". From my understanding she never left. In a way I wish I had known the whole story, but I know how most of our stories turn out; it's not pretty.

I have some good news to share with you today. My Grandmama is here for a visit and I am loving it! She is the same grandmother I spoke of earlier in the book. I haven't talked to her about any of this, or about my first marriage, until she got here. She is proud of what I am doing and how I am growing as a person. Yes, I realize most grandmothers say they are proud of their grandchildren, but my Grandma really means what she says. She is a no nonsense gal that I love so very much. I am sure you are all wondering why I did not turn to my Grandmother when things got bad. I don't have a good answer for that. I think by the time all was said and done that I just felt so darn alone and helpless. I was all the way in Texas and my Grandmother was up in Michigan with hardships of her own. As much as I know in my heart that she would have carried my burden until I could stand alone; she didn't need all my baggage. My Grandmamma is here for two whole weeks. I will laugh with her, cry with her, and bake goodies that are not good for us with her. I am so thankful for her, our relationship as grandmother and grandchild, and our friendship. My Grandma ROCKS!

I am on the backside of a whirlwind two weeks with my Grandmother and the long ride to take her back home to Michigan. Why am I telling you this? I am writing a little filler because I have random thoughts about nothing this morning and I know it is due to Grandma's visit and the crazy long drive back home. So, I figured I would share a bit about my two week visit with grandma and about the trip to get her out here to New Hampshire and back to Michigan. I realize it has absolutely nothing to do with domestic violence, but as I said before, "not everything can be about sadness, tears, and stuff like that". Okay, I am paraphrasing, but I am not about to go back and find exactly what words I typed ages ago; you all get my meaning. Not to mention the fact I cannot write an entire book about my visit with Grandma, and it will be a nice break from the ugly crud I am normally writing about.

During the first week in May, my grandmother decided she wanted to hop on a train and come out here for a visit (my grandmother is just shy of eighty-four). Once my husband read her train schedule he said, "We'll drive out to get Grandma. She is not taking that train ride." That phone conversation with my husband about my grandmother's trip turned into a quick 17+ hour drive out to Michigan to get her. First though, I had to scramble around here to thoroughly clean the house, deal with our pets, and drag a full sized futon up two flights of stairs and into the second bedroom (hubby helped with the last bit). So, on Friday night my husband picked up his twelve year old son and we took off for Michigan. Our trip out there was pretty uneventful; thank God; and we pulled into her drive around noon on Saturday. We spent the night, packed Grandma into the van the next day, and headed back for New Hampshire. Again, an uneventful road trip, thank God.

Okay, a side road to my side road... FYI, my first husband would NEVER have decided to jump in our vehicle and go grab my grandmother from Michigan, so she could spend two weeks with me and the rest of the family. (Though, I highly doubt he would even donate blood if he knew it would save the life of one of my family members.) Then again, I am not sure if my grandmother would have wanted to stay with us. She tried it twice before and my then-husband was not the most hospitable of hosts to her. Anyways, my point is this: WHY THE HELL DID I SPEND SO MANY YEARS WITH MR. OBVIOUSLY WRONG FOR ME AND NOT WITH THE BEAUTIFUL MAN I HAVE NOW? I know all good things come in time, but I really wish I would have met my current husband before I had met, and married, my abuser. I suppose though if I had done that then I wouldn't be writing this little book for you ladies. Funny how life works out, no?

I had plans to work on my manuscript during any down time I might have had while Grandma was visiting; that didn't happen. A few days before we went to pick up my grandmother my computer decided to do a massive nose dive. For a blind woman, who uses her computer as a life line to the outside world, this sucked in a major way! I tried working on my book, but half the time I couldn't hear my screen reader and the other half of the time I thought I had hit the wrong keys and deleted my writing. Where was I going with this? Oh!! My point was that even though I was not able to work on my manuscript, I was able to catch up on some seriously needed "us time" with Grandma.

We got back here to New Hampshire late Sunday night and spent the first couple of days catching up. The first thing I did to celebrate Grandma being with us was to bake her a cake she had never had before. It was awesome to bake a treat for her instead of the other way around. To cure the curiosity of those who love junk food; I made a white layered cake with sliced strawberries, blueberries, and whipped topping in the center and then frosted the whole cake with the remaining whipped topping. My grandmother used to grow those kinds of berries in her garden, so I thought she would love the cake; she did. From there we packed in a trip to Connecticut to see two of my three children; which included an adventure to the beach, a Sunday service, a four mile walk for hunger, an early surprise birthday party for Grandma (on second thought, maybe this could be its own book), a motorcycle ride with my husband which was all her idea, a morning of volunteering at my church's food pantry, a night out with my brother (who ran in a road race for our grandmother), a hike up one of the large rocks that seems so oddly placed in our city, a birthday party for Grandma's first great great-grandchild, and a little sit down so my husband could help Grandma put all the photos she wanted to keep on to a DVD she could take home. Now squeeze in there that my grandmother threw me into the Lion's Baking Den to learn how to make cinnamon rolls from scratch and home made apple pie with a freshly made crust! All that for a gal hinging on eighty- four years of age; not too shabby.

As I said before, our trip out to get Grandma was not that eventful; the ride to take her back was though. We got everything packed into the van and managed to make it partly through New York before a cop decided to pull us over for speeding. Can you imagine my grandmother being awakened in the middle of the night by a damn flashlight shining in her face? I am so perturbed about the whole affair because my husband was clearly going with the speed of traffic and the only reason the cop stopped us was because we had an out of state plate on our van. Here we were with all these New Yorkers flying passed us as we sat on the side of the highway getting a ticket. You have no idea how bad I would like to write that officer a nice note telling him how wrong I feel he was for targeting an out of state vehicle. My husband is not about to take two days off from work to drive to New York to fight a stupid ticket and that cop knew that. Is that how New York cops roll when trying to meet their end of the month quota for moving violations? I am disgusted! I am sure I will be upsetting any New York official that reads this, but when I read article after article about how that part of New York's roadways are handled when it comes to speeding tickets, I don't care who I tick off. I am beginning to wonder if the phrase "Highway Robbery" comes from there.

Anyways, we got Grandma home just after 11:30 in the morning on Saturday, spent the night, and were outta there by 7:00 the next morning. By the grace of God we made it back through New York without incident. You would think they would be happy with the load of money they make from collecting tolls that they wouldn't need their officers going after out of state drivers in the middle of the night, but apparently not. My husband says I am slowly picking away at the list of states we are welcome in (New York and Connecticut thus far) and I like to say I am narrowing down our choices for a state I want to retire to...

Now that I have my grandmother's trip off my chest, I guess I will start in on a few things that I said were random thoughts running through my head. I consider these random thoughts because I don't think I would debate any of them to anyone except myself. As I am sure you can probably tell by now, from reading the previous pages, that I am a thinker, a talker, a philosophizer, and hypothesizer. I stress that last label because no one truly knows or understands the mind of an abuser, and so we must take mental leaps. It is during these many mental leaps that we also hypothesize as to why we, as the abused, put up with all the heartache that we do and pick such "lovely" choices to be our significant others.

Random Thought # 1:

Why we don't run to the police I have had numerous conversations with non-abused people who ask the same question, "Why didn't you go to the police?". Before I give the answer to that question, let me say this… If you have never been on the receiving end of domestic violence, no amount of explaining to you will make you understand what the abused woman goes through. We abused ladies have seen the system fail in one capacity or another. First off, do you have any idea what the price tag is for a restraining order? Not to mention the fact that most of us are victims of financial abuse, have no money of our own, and have no flipping support system that can lend us the funds required to procure said restraining order. Even if we manage to work out the issue with being able to pay for the restraining order, there is now the hurdle of making our way to the courthouse without our abuser finding out. If you think a simple phone call will bring our Fairy Godmother, with a restraining order in hand, to our door, then you are sadly mistaken. Here is where the non-abused pipes up and says, "Then call the police the next time he lays a hand on you!" Here is the problem with that, and I know most of you have seen an episode or two of COPS; we call the cops, they may or may not arrest our abuser, he may or may not be put in jail for a "hard core one nighter" in the joint, and then our abuser is right back in our face. How the hell do you expect an abused woman to get her butt out of Dodge in one night? We don't have the legal right to change the locks or, God forbid, displace our abuser if his name is on the lease of where we are residing. Yup, our abuser still has rights and we feel abused by the system…

What non-abused people call a grocery list of excuses on our part, we call insurmountable hurdles. I am sure there isn't one abused lady out there that wouldn't love to have faith in our police officers and courts, but nothing is perfect. So, let's say now that we are lucky enough to have our abuser arrested, if only for one night, and we scramble to the courthouse before he is released to obtain a restraining order; what then? It isn't like a few pieces of paper are going to become this protective shield against our abuser once he comes back to our place of residence to beat us for calling the cops in the first place. We abused ladies live in fear day in and day out. We don't see any light at the end of the tunnel and we believe that each day could be the last day we take a breath. A restraining order does not erase that fear; doesn't even come close. Am I beginning to paint a clear picture of what it is like to be the abused to those who have no clue about what it means to walk in our shoes? It is so darn easy for those who have never been abused to sit back and, well basically, interrogate us on why we didn't run head long into the nearest police station or courthouse. It is also this mentality of the non-abused that prevents us from trusting in the system. Granted, no one in their right mind would want to be abused. But, after the first few nasty names and punches, what abused woman IS in their right mind anymore?

Random Thought # 2:

Abused women who cry for help, but don't take it What I am about to write will sound like an attack on battered women; it's not. I am going to play Devil's advocate for any family member who tried to help, but then were turned down by the very abused lady that pleaded for said help. I am going to say, right off the bat, that most of us abused women truly aren't thinking clearly. I know I am asking a lot of the family member who tries to save their daughter or sister or cousin or whatever, but hang in there. Remember, I am putting myself (an abused woman) in the shoes of our family members or close friends, so don't even think this is a personal attack. Though if you are one of the gals I am about to go off about, then read what I type repeatedly until you realize you need to snap out of whatever pity party you are having for yourself.

Do any of you abused ladies know what you are putting your family members or friends or co-workers through when you go crying to them for help, but then don't take any help or advice they try to give you? I am only going off about this because there are hundreds of thousands of battered ladies who would give their left arm for just one person to listen and try to help get them away from their abuser. Look at it from the stand point of the person you are shedding countless tears to… You dump all of it into their lap, beg for help, and then toss that life line right back at them. What are you thinking? How often do you think you can cry on a family member's or friend's shoulder about how abused you are before they just stop listening to anything you have to say? I truly believe many abused women do this sort of thing to those that try to help them merely for the attention value. At home they are abused, but while crying over a cup of coffee with someone they trust they get sympathy and understanding and support. The problem is you seem so darn sincere to the person trying to help

SURVIVING DOMESTIC VIOLENCE

you that they really think you will leave your abuser if they can help you do so.

The sad thing is that these type of abused women will never take the help offered to them and then will only go on the attack against any person who decides enough is enough and they refuse to listen to the belly aching. Honestly, that is just what is going on during these situations; belly aching. This right here is a clear case of insanity! Abused woman cries for help, abused woman gets help offered, abused woman turns away help, abused woman cries for help... It is completely crazy! Or what about those abused women who cry to a relative and then verbally attack that same relative for taking their side or saying negative things about their abuser? Want my two cents worth of advice? If you are abused and go to someone for help; you better be prepared to accept that help!

It is abused ladies like you that run the crazy hamster wheel of insanity who make it harder for those of us who truly want and need the help to ask for it. Battered ladies that get to this point of hair pulling craziness should be treated like a drug addict who swears they want help while they are shooting the crap into their arm or snorting it up their nose or inhaling it into their lungs. The only way to get even remotely through to those type of abused women is for an intervention to take place, you physically remove the gal from her environment, and then watch them like a hawk. Why? Because those ladies will run back to their abuser like a drug addict to their drug pusher. It is just so sad and maddening at the same time for anyone who tries to help those in need. I suppose, like with drug addicts; your family member or friend will need to hit rock bottom before accepting the help for real. Only problem with that is there is a good chance rock bottom means either a trip to the emergency room or morgue.

Random Thought # 3:

Opposites attract I need to get this "Opposites Attract" thing out of my system today. Yes, it is a good thing if we find a mate with some differences in personality to ours, but I highly suggest not running train wreck fast into a man that is a complete polar opposite of yourself; there are limits. If we involved ourselves with a mirror image of us, then we would never learn and grow with our significant other and the relationship would become stagnant; we don't want that. Going for someone on the very other end of the spectrum we are on can cause a lot more trouble for us than it is worth though. See, if this whole premise is true about opposites attracting, then we who are prone to become an abuse victim will only attract those who are prone to be an abuser. What is the good in that? I say if you don't have the basic, but deep rooted, things in common then for the love of all things good in this world don't start a relationship with that person!

I should have known right from the get go that my relationship with my first husband would lead to a violent one. We had absolutely nothing in common; nothing! I love art and I am not sure if he can even hold a paint brush the right way. I appreciate a good sporting event; even though I have my favorites; and he acts like he is a monetary shareholder in his favorite teams. I love to read just about any book I can get my hands on and I doubt he would read anything more evolved than nudity and rag mags. I believe in the Lord and enjoy church and he would only use the Lord's name in vain or step foot in a church if it made him look good to the public. I put the welfare of others before I do myself and he only thinks about himself. I crazy enjoy picnics and walks and the woods while he enjoys money and money and more money. These were all things I knew about him within the first few months, but yet I stuck around instead of running. I went to college to earn my degrees in Criminal Justice and Liberal Arts and instead I earned a degree in Domestic Violence; the hard way no less. So long story short, find someone you have enough in common with that makes the prospect of growing old with them fun and not work. Also make sure that same someone has enough differences than you so they can get you to try new things and live life to the fullest. It may seem like a difficult task, but it is much easier when you know exactly what you don't want in your Forever Man.

Random Thought # 4:

We marry our fathers I can safely say I want this theory squashed like a nasty bug before it gets the chance to jump out of the hopper and become an actual law! Who in their right mind would even fathom that marrying our father's clone would be a "good thing"? Maybe it would be a nice theory if we ladies all had great loving fathers that put us on a pedestal and what not, but we don't. This theory has such a fine line. I don't think we could ever find a man that was like our father, if our father was a good one. It seems that those women who attract the "just like my father type" end up looking for Daddy because their father was never there for them or find the guy exactly like their father and wind up being abused just like they were as a child. Get why this is so messed up? If we have an awesome father while growing up, then he will teach us to run from the first guy we swear is the right one for us. Don't marry your father; listen to him. If your father meets the love of your life and offers you a way out; take it! The odds are your father is right about the guy you brought home for him to meet and sometimes finding that fact out for yourself years later could prove to be too late.

What I am finding out with my current husband is that he is so much like my brother and favorite uncle. No, that is not weird at all, so stop acting like you got the Willies from that last sentence. My husband is the same age as my brother; positive number one. My husband likes motorcycle rides just like my brother and uncle; positive number two. My husband shares a similar sense of humor as my brother and uncle do; positive number three. My husband has a passion for camping and fishing just like my uncle does; positive number four. I could go on and on, but am hoping you get the picture. It is important to see how your potential Forever Man interacts with your family. Does he ignore them; does he refuse to hang out with your family with you; does he verbally bash them when they are not around… And whatever you do, don't pick a man that treats his mother horribly or too lovingly. Otherwise he'll end up treating you just as horribly or will treat you like you could never be as "perfect" as his mommy is. The whole relationship between a boy and his mommy is a freaky one if you choose the wrong boy to become involved with. Case in point; my first husband treats his mother like crud unless he wants something from her. If you go saying one bad word about her though, you had better be prepared for the wrath to come down upon you! That relationship is completely unhealthy… Don't get me started. Again, a fine line…

Some of you reading this maybe thinking that a Forever Man is the last thing to do on your To Do List, but none the less we have to discuss his potential introduction into your life. Yes, the healing process for you must be top priority. Yes, your children (if you have any) are top priority as well. But, after you have worked on yourself, have worked on becoming a better mom, have worked to put the baggage you were carrying out to the curb for trash day; you still deserve true love. Don't expect to be completely recovered from the Hell you went through before Prince Pretty Damn Close enters your life. He maybe coming into your life to help with what is left of you. I am not saying to chase down your Forever Man at the bar or church or statewide auction. I am saying to make yourself ready and open for the poor man to have a fighting chance. If we do not allow ourselves to find lasting love, then that is just going to be another win for our abuser.

Granted, none of this is a game for us, but it is for our abuser and all he wants to do is win.

Believe me, trying to even talk to a man was crazy difficult for me. Let's face it… Our abuser has made us scared of anything with testicles. I trusted my brother and nephews when I first got up here and no one else. I was petrified to even ride in the same vehicle as my mobility therapist! I had to come to the realization that I would not get the help I needed as a blind person if I didn't put my trust in the man who would teach me to feel good about walking outdoors. Once I felt comfortable with him I became comfortable around my brother's former brother in-law. I added one male at a time until I felt comfortable enough to talk somewhat freely around one that I wasn't related to in some way, shape, or form. It was nice to talk with a man about music, poetry, families, and past relationships. My mother was right about one thing… Every lady should have at least one male best friend. I just happened to marry mine!

Did I make it easy for him to enter into my life, I don't think so. Do I have my moments that place him in the middle of a nasty flashback, yes. Do I ever make him pay for the sins of my once abuser, I pray not. Does he know everything that happened during my first marriage, no. Do I truly love him, yes. Am I crazy in love with him, undoubtedly. Would I regret my life with him if it were cut short, no. Every day that passed me by, while in my first marriage, seemed to crawl so slowly that I thought it would never end. Sad, praying for a day to end, but resenting the fact another day will begin and your existence remains the same. Now I am enjoying all that comes along with my current husband and time is just flying by us. Before there were too many hours in the day and now there just aren't enough. There aren't enough hours to love him, to laugh with him, to bicker with him, to allow him to bring out my full potential as a woman or friend or wife or lover.

What I have with my husband is something I pray all battered women find with another human being. I can't allow myself to believe we abused women went through all the torment just to come out of it without love. We deserve all the love our close family members want to give us, our bestest of friends want to give us, and another person will eventually want to intimately give us. We go for so long being told, and then reminded, that we do not deserve even the simplest form of love or kindness from another. Please do not let your abuser feel he has triumphed over you by not opening your heart for family and friends and, eventually, a significant other. It is your abuser who is incapable of real love, not you. It is your abuser who does not deserve true happiness, not you. It is your abuser who should merely exist while you show the world you can shine! Stand up ladies and be counted...

Random Thought # 5:

How would an abuser comfort an abused child? Here is a good fucking question for all you abusive pigs out there living in your own world of selfishness... How would you comfort your child if you found out their husband or wife or significant other was brutally abusing them? I mean, after all you are the very reason they grew up thinking it was alright to be another person's punching bag and/or door mat in the first place! Though maybe you are so self-absorbed that seeing your child abused and hurting wouldn't remind you at all of what a pig you are/were to their own mother; maybe.

Would you honestly be able to sit there, while your child cried on your shoulder, and say it is wrong to hurt another human being; the abuser should be locked away; you will protect them; so on and so on and so on? Wouldn't that make you somewhat of a hypocrite? Or would you be afraid to listen to your abused child because you would be running the risk of the child asking you why you beat their mom and yelled at their mom and/or cheated on their mom? Kids will ALWAYS do what they see their parents doing and not do what they are told; it's part of being a kid. So, the odds are very good that boys will see their father beat their mom and think it is okay to do that. The odds are also very good for a daughter to see her mother being pounded on and think that is what true love is. I am glad I am not with my children's father anymore! I'll be able to tell my children that abuse is wrong and allowing yourself to be abused is wrong. Can the abuser say the same thing with a straight face; doubt it.

Random Thought # 6:

What do abusers see when they look at us? So, what exactly do our abusers see when they look at us during a fit of rage? All abused ladies know the look; glazed over eyes that are full of rage and a flushed face, but what is going on behind that glazed expression? Do you abusers even see us or do you see a punching bag, a fucked up childhood courtesy of your mommy, a past girlfriend that did you wrong, a reminder of the mistakes you make on a daily basis, what what what! I'd really like to know because the only picture I hold in my memory of my first husband is that glazed over intense look of rage. You know, the look that makes you want to pee your pants, run in fright, curl up and die; that look. Just so you get my point, once abuser of mine, I have no good memories of your face at all. No memories of when you were actually a happy person. No memories of you looking lovingly into my eyes. No memories of the pure love you may have had for each one of our children. I only have memories of a man full of rage, hate, and God knows whatever else made you look like you bordered on the edge of insanity. Are all abusers eyes full of that same ugliness? The ugliness us abused ladies know in our hearts we did not create? What is it that you see because I know it isn't me. It isn't your wife or girlfriend... It isn't the mother of your children... It isn't the lady you confess to love... What is it?

I suppose this will be another question we abused ladies will have to add to the lengthy list of questions we have for our abusers. We'll never know what our abusers see when they come after us during a fit of rage. It is like they become some different beast that doesn't care who you are or how much pain he puts you through. Oh no, this isn't a way out for our abusers to proclaim, "But I swear I had no idea what I was doing at the time". I may never understand what drives a man to brutalize the woman in his life, but I do understand how those same women can describe her abusers eyes with such detail. I haven't seen my once abuser's eyes since 1998, but my mind's vision is very clear when I dredge up the memory of his enraged face and clenched fists.

I am beginning to realize that after I get all of this abuse crud out of my system that I may have to begin anew with a book about the aftermath of divorce. No, not the typical stuff of how to survive divorce... I am talking about all the other stuff you never figure will effect your life. I am talking about having to put up with crud from your ex, having to put up with crud from your ex's new squeeze, having to put up with your ex in-laws, and all of that sort of thing. With all the things I have had to listen to over the past four plus years, I should have a ton to put into print. And since I become very sarcastic when having to put up with my ex and his extended family, this should be a fun project. I can laugh at it now and make jokes, but it really is annoying and even heart-wrenching at times. I get tired of having to put up with drama brought on by others and think it will soon be time to let that out and let it go. The only problem I see with that is the fact that even when I accomplish letting it go, they will just keep up with the garbage they sling. So, wouldn't their behavior be constituted as some form of mental dysfunction? They are continually doing the same thing and getting the same result (no control over me). You would think ex's and their families would have better things to do with their time, but nope... I was stupid enough to think that once the divorce was final that I wouldn't have to deal with a lot of the drama; I was wrong. My ex is still controlling, he married a woman who is just as controlling, and his mother needs to play the control game. Is there no end? I'll stop though about this topic because it really isn't meant for this here book.

I wouldn't even feel compelled to bring it up if certain people would just leave me the heck alone. Just because you (and you all know who you are) use the children to make nasty digs at me or try to control or manipulate things, doesn't make it right. You got what you wanted; me gone... I am learning that abusing me wasn't enough, cheating on me wasn't enough, kicking me out and forcing me to leave the kids wasn't enough. Now you and your lovely bride feel it necessary to put our children through Hell just so you can try to hurt me. Let me shed some light on what you are doing... IT ISN'T WORKING! All you are accomplishing is to make our children mad at you and your bride. Don't either of you care that a few years from now the kids may want absolutely nothing to do with either one of you? You guys can't control the children forever, ya know. I have begged you though to stop that ugly behavior and all you did was basically laugh me off. What are you both so angry about that you feel the need to control kids or manipulate those around you? It is really pathetic and sad...

So where do we go from here? Since this whole thing started as a journal of release, over four years ago, I am not sure if it will ever have an ending. It's cast of characters still go on with their lives while we, as potential survivors of domestic violence, try desperately to make sense of all the madness. I know it isn't fair that we abused women get left holding the bag of negativity while those who abused us move on like nothing happened, but that is the reality of it all. I am sorry this is how it ends up turning out, but it doesn't have to stay that way forever.

Once you have decided to escape from the abusive relationship you are in, you will get a new lease on life. This new lease will come with, what seems, a steep price. You will have your days when you feel you can't get out of bed. You'll have your days when you just can't eat. You'll have your nights where you can't sleep. Basically, you will run the same gamut of emotions as you did while you were in the abusive relationship. There is a big difference though… YOU AND ONLY YOU CAN DECIDE HOW YOUR STORY PLAYS OUT! Do you truly want to be a survivor of domestic violence or do you just want to exist in this world? I know surviving is hard, very damn hard, but to get out of an abusive relationship without a new perspective on how life could be is so much worse.

We abused women spent too many years just walking through life in a haze. We merely existed while life passed us by. When you are involved in an abusive relationship, you forget what is outside of your world of pain. Even if we have children, we are still basically doing everything on automatic pilot. What choice do we have? If we don't run our day to day existence like that, we would all crack under the weight of it all and lose any grasp on reality we had left. I bet a lot of you often wondered at the end of the day how you accomplished all that you did around your abuser's castle or with the children. I actually get a creepy tingle up my spine when I look back at my thirteen plus years in Hell. I truly don't know how I did it without major thoughts of suicide.

I think, no I know… I know what made me wake up every morning, put my feet on the floor, and stomach another abusive day. It was my three beautiful children. They knew I was sad even when I tried so hard to hide it. My oldest son is sharper than he lets on and he often asked questions I really didn't want to answer.

My daughter (the middle child) feels emotions to the extreme and, I know, took on some of the pain I was feeling. My youngest just wanted to hug and kiss his momma until all her sadness was gone. No matter what their father put me through, I couldn't bring myself to bad mouth him to our children. Besides, their father was doing a good enough job on his own. Where was I going with all of this? Oh, my children… Watching them grow day in and day out, into little adults, made me realize that I didn't just want to exist. I took a hard look at my reality and decided that wasn't what I wanted for my three children. They saw me slowly dying inside and what kind of mother is that for them to have? I kicked myself everyday that went by and the kids saw me fade away. I wished for so long that I could have done things differently for them, but I couldn't change the past.

I am changing my future though, and hopefully theirs in the process. They now see a mom full of life, happiness, and love. I am a much better mom now that I am free to be the woman I was meant to be before all of their father's abuse of me. They see me with my current husband and, I pray, see that is what a real loving relationship should be. Husbands and wives love each other. Partners love each other. Parents and children love each other. Friends love each other. Families love each other. True love comes with no strings attached and that is what I pray my children understand. I am not saying my side of the family is perfect, but they show unconditional love and that is what is important in this life.

I honestly can't imagine how hard it would be for a woman, who has no children to draw strength from, to be involved in an abusive relationship. I thank God as often as I can for my two knights in shining armor and my saving grace. They made me see the difference between existing and living. Now that I know the difference, what about you ladies? Do you want to go through this life existing or actually living? That is almost as hard of a question to answer as it is to answer the question about being a survivor or victim of domestic violence. Oh, sorry, we can answer the question easily enough. It is putting that answer into action that is so darn scary.

I know once you have gone so many crazy years consumed by abuse that it is hard to realize there is something more than just existing day to day. After all, it was the defense mechanism of merely existing that got us through the abuse as well as we did. Deciding to exist is like wrapping ourselves up in a warm blanket of protection. It is this blanket of protection that allowed us to become desensitized to much of the abuse. In a way that was a good thing and in a way that was a bad thing. Existing was your shield against abuse while you were in the abusive relationship, but now it is just another obstacle you need to get around in order to regain a hold on your life and the brilliant woman you were before all the nightmares started.

Getting passed existing, and learning to live, is that new lease on life I was talking about earlier. It will be rough at first, but so worth it in the end. It is so hard to say when I went from existing to living. The changes are so subtle and take awhile, so you don't even realize it is going on. One morning you wake up and think, "Oh great, another flipping day", but then that turns into waking up one morning and saying to yourself, "Man, the birds singing out my window sound amazing!". It is the difference between eating nothing for breakfast and enjoying a bagel while reading the paper or watching the news. It is the difference between taking in oxygen to maintain life and deeply inhaling the aroma of a midnight summer's eve. We forgot about all of these daily miracles and creature comforts because we spent so long as mistreated slaves and for what? Ladies, we paid whatever dues karma felt we needed to pay while going through all the abuse. Once you get out of that situation; grab the bull by the horns and

SURVIVING DOMESTIC VIOLENCE

live! We owe it to ourselves to live. We owe it to any lady, who never got out of her own abusive relationship, to live. We owe it to our children (if we have any) to live. And, if we believe in a Higher Power, we owe it to them to live and show a new appreciation for the gift we have been given. All of us already spent way too long in a Hell created by our abuser. Why on Earth should we keep that Hell going? Live ladies, live!!

The last few paragraphs make me sound like I am on some soapbox don't they? Well, maybe I am. I can't stress enough how important it is to remove the shackles placed on us by our abuser AND doing whatever it takes to keep them off. Yes, relapses will occur, and we must deal with them, but they will slowly lessen and fade. Now please don't misinterpret me when I say "doing whatever it takes". I am not suggesting you envelope yourselves in a haze full of booze and pills; they won't do anything for you, but keep the pain at bay for awhile. I am saying to let it all out and let it all go. We don't want to mask the abuse we endured by abusing ourselves with booze or drugs or putting our bodies out for sex'capades. The latter means jumping from one unhealthy bed of a relationship to another and another and another in hopes to find the "love" you are so desperately craving. None of those things make any sense. Why would any woman want to get out of an abusive relationship to only turn around and abuse herself? There are so many other ways, healthy ways, to rid each and every cell in your body of the pain.

You ladies have options while you walk on the path of healing and I think right now is a good time to list a few of those alternatives to the obvious alcohol and drug oblivion. I am not saying to run the spectrum of options. I am not saying all of these options listed help everyone. I am not saying these are the only options you have. My intention is to make you aware of what is out there for you and that you do not have to go through your recovery alone; never... I truly felt in my heart that when I got up here to New Hampshire that I was going to be alone on my way to recovering from the abusive relationship I was in. Feeling that way; I turned to the one thing I knew would take the pain away, if only for a few hours. I turned to bourbon and Sprite; a lovely drink my first husband introduced me to. No, I didn't drink everyday. I didn't even drink every week. Every so often my ex-abuser would do something to turn me into the cowering mutt he swore I was and I had three tall drinks. I would drink and then I would write. That is why I didn't keep any of my original writings for this book. It wasn't that I was too drunk to type straight. It was because my writing was so full of hatred and rage and just about every other word was a swear word. It took me a good three or four months to realize that the alcohol was keeping me trapped and not setting me free. So, I beg all of you ladies to choose wisely how to bring yourself out of the funk you might be feeling. I can't imagine what I would have done if I had to also battle alcoholism along with recovering from abuse…

Option One: Domestic violence support groups

I do highly recommend you visit one of these groups. I believe each woman walks away from one of these support meetings with a different outlook. As you know, I went to some of these meetings; every Tuesday. What I noticed with my group was that some women wallowed in self-pity, some wanted to move forward and had in-laws like mine trying to keep them down, and some ladies refused to say a single word. Personally, I walked away from my group knowing I didn't want to end up like some of the ladies who pitied themselves and with the knowledge that I was not alone. Granted, I wasn't about to lean on any of these women, but they made me come to the realization that I could. I am just really hesitant about taking advice or getting any real support from ladies who are still addicted to their abuse; it's not healthy.

What I also walked away with from my group was the idea of writing my journal of all the major abuse I endured by the hands of my first husband. It is the very journal I put into the book earlier; no changes. I tried to make the journal as cut and dry as possible; devoid of emotion. This allowed me to let it out, let it go, and feel like it happened to someone else. It was difficult at first, but got easier and easier. Writing all that happened to me made me realize that it was in the past and that I would take steps to ensure it would never happen again. I do recommend writing in a journal like the one I did. I DO NOT suggest that you revisit the journal over and over again. Doing that could result in self-pity. Get it all out, read over it, and either lock it away until you know it could help another abused woman or burn it to celebrate your new found freedom.

Option Two: Visiting a place of worship

Before you ladies shy away from this option, at least listen to what I have to say on the matter. I am not saying to run out and hug the nearest religious tree you can find. Some places of worship or religious groups run the risk of being the kind to brainwash a wounded soul and you need to stay clear of those. What I am suggesting is to find a place of worship, that you find comforting, and enjoy the fellowship it can offer you. You don't have to be a religious person or even a spiritual one to enjoy fellowship. Fellowship allows you to interact with other people in a non-threatening environment and that is a major part of entering a world full of folks. Since most fellowship revolves around coffee and food, there is little risk that you will be outed as a domestic violence survivor until you are ready to say something. You also don't run the risk of joining the "Poor Me Club" of booze hounds at your local bar. It is all about interaction... Listen to the older folks discuss life or politics or how young people are out of control. Sit back and watch the little ones fight and laugh and play and inevitably cry. It is life you are watching and you are in a safe environment.

I went to one church with my current husband (then boyfriend) and literally fell asleep during the service. I sat there, trying to fight off sleep, thinking that if I wrote my name down on a guest card that these folks would hunt me down and suck me in. I didn't want any of that! I waited a couple of months and tried another church. I am now a member of that very church and have been baptized into the only religion I have known since the age of about six. I grew up loving the church because it was a safe haven from a hostile childhood, but then I lost that safe haven when I married my first husband. Going to church was out of the question and didn't fit into my first husband's insanely "busy" Sundays. Not to mention that I was beaten down so much that I truly felt I did not deserve the love of the Lord. Man, it is amazing how abuse can effect every aspect of your life… Even though I am a member of my church, and have a few nice relationships with some folks, I do not talk about my abuse. I am there to forget my abuse. I am there to help lift others up during their times of trouble. I am there to rejoice in their celebrations. Good or bad, the people of my church remind me that life goes on; love goes on…

Option Three: Pen and paper

Your task, when you are ready to tackle it, is to repair your soul, your mind, and your body. You may not think that each one is linked to the other, but they are. Once I felt safe in my environment and in my own head, I began to write. I had gotten the journal out of the way and was beginning to crank out poetry and song lyrics. No, I just didn't decide to become a poet or lyricist out of nowhere; silly… I have been writing poetry since around the same time I found my first church and music has always been a huge part of my life. Again, all that was squashed during my first marriage, but renewed itself in full force once I was free! I found I could write a poem or song about my abuser and know I wouldn't get hurt in any way for how I felt. It wasn't always about my anger for my abuser though. My writing slowly turned from "how could you" stuff to "it's not

my fault and I can't fix you" stuff. I was evolving, I was growing, I was returning to the woman I thought was dead.

When I met my current husband, my writing took on another look. I wasn't putting all my thoughts and feelings of rage and sadness into a poem or song about my once abuser. After all I thought, "Why am I spending so much time on a person who feels he did nothing wrong and refuses to change?". Instead, I began writing about my budding feelings for the new man in my life. I spent way too many years not being allowed to voice my opinions or feelings that opening up to the man I was falling in love with was, to me, insane. So, I took the safe way out and wrote and wrote and wrote. All that writing encouraged me to analyze what I wanted, and didn't want, out of my new life and out of a new relationship. It was crazy therapeutic! I went from writing about the man I loved, to allowing him to read what I wrote, to allowing him to love me. I now look back at all of the poetry and lyrics I wrote and rejoice in the progress I have made and am still making.

Option Four: Working Out

As I said before; our soul, mind, and body are linked. If one of the three are unhealthy, then the others are unhealthy. The working out for me actually came first. Our bodies are so overwhelmed with emotion, that exists in every cell, and we need to get it out of our bodies through exercise and a lot of sweat. If we don't feel safe enough to talk about how we feel or believe writing our words down just isn't doing the trick, then running on a treadmill or lifting a few weights in a local fitness center can do the job. If you don't feel comfortable going out in public yet, then purchase a piece of exercise equipment for your home. Get the body moving ladies and shed all those negative words heaped upon you for years and years!

Because I am blind, and just can't jump in the car and drive to a fitness center whenever I want to, I purchased and put together my own elliptical machine. I used that when unable to get to the gym with my brother. After awhile I tried dragging my older sister to the gym. When I realized that was not such a hot idea, I asked my mobility therapist to teach me how to get around my gym without a sight guide. I went through all of that and got the nerve to ask for a male trainer. Wow, what a rebel against abuse! I worked out at that gym until I moved to the city I reside in now. I am back to working out on equipment in my home, but have added camping and hiking during the warmer months to my exercise routine. My brother is a runner and I would love to get into the groove of running once I deal with those female issues I discussed quite a few pages back. My point in all of this ladies is to get off your ass; skinny or otherwise; and purge your body of all the negativity. Hell, curse under your breath with every step on the stair master or with every weight you lift. It works amazingly well. Once your body begins to rid itself of all the nastiness, your mind and soul will follow suit; I promise.

Option Five: Seek therapy

I will admit up front that this was not an option for me. I, unfortunately, have seen too many therapists that don't work and heard too many stories of therapists that don't work. I do believe that therapy only works for those willing to share everything and want to make a permanent change in their lives. I get annoyed with the counselors that just want the money from their attention seeking patients that they will either not treat them properly or will feed into the "tragedy" of what their patient says is going on in their lives. I also don't care for the therapist who figures bottles of mood behavior pills are the cure all. I have made my point, I think, crystal clear earlier in my writing. I should probably not go on the attack of therapists now. But again, if you are not the type of therapist I am describing, then you will not take any offense to what I write.

I have no doubt among all the bad therapists that there are some good ones. I would not make a good therapist. I don't think I would have the patience to listen to someone who is running on the hamster wheel of craziness, yet refuses to take the help offered to them. So, if you do choose to seek out a therapist; make sure they are a no nonsense kind of one. Do you want a therapist who will only mask your pain with pill after pill or one that will help you make major life changes to enrich your life and rid you of the pain? If you do not like your therapist then keep looking until you find one you do or decide therapy is not the avenue for you. Keep your options open though. Don't allow my negative comments about a few bad apple therapists hinder you from finding yourself a doozy of a one. Another thing… if you find a good therapist that tells you to trash anything in your life that is harmful, negative, or abusive in nature; listen to them for the love of God! Good therapists like this are like the family members who try desperately to get you away from your abusive relationship. After awhile though if you don't listen to the advice or take the help, then like the family member, the therapist will give up on you and send you to another professional. Another long story short… don't seek therapy unless you are darn good and ready to accept the truth and the help. See why I wouldn't make a good therapist?

I need to finally change out of my fuzzy robe and ballet slippers into something more presentable. What do you expect though? I roll out of bed, get my husband off to work, grab a cup of java, and then climb the stairs up to my computer. I forget that I actually need to dress or shower or brush my teeth until it is late in the day and all my thoughts are typed out of my system. Be right back. Since I mentioned writing, I think I will pull out some of my stuff for you ladies to read. Primping first though. I don't want to have to answer my front door in the garb I am wearing at this very moment…

I am back, after a quick twenty minute primping, and feel much better. Though I am running sockless. I have two pairs of bootie socks that have colors around the ankle and, unfortunately, can't tell them apart. So, no socks until my hubby can fill me in on which ones match. Surprisingly, as a blind woman, it is the simple things like socks that are the hardest on me. Oh, I was taught to label this and label that and so on and so on, but let's face it… I have to be the laziest blind person I know when it comes to doing things the blind person way! Okay, back to my point about dragging out some writings of mine for you to read… Since most of my poetry is on my old hard drive, I will let you read a set of lyrics I wrote about my first husband and some I wrote about my current husband before he even proposed to me. I am sure you'll be able to detect which song is about which man, and for reference, I love country music and you'll have to use that frame of mind while reading my stuff. Oh, what the heck… I'll even toss in some lyrics I wrote after realizing clinging to an abusive past would only kill me in more ways than one…

P.S. I write all my stuff with capital letters and the least amount of punctuation possible; just a warning. Well, here we go and I hope you enjoy what I have written. If anything, I am sure a few of you reading this will be able to relate to the words I type.

TAKING MY HEART WHEN I LEAVE
by L. A. Burnett

TAKE THE CAR—TAKE THE HOUSE—TAKE THE FURNITURE IN IT—TAKE THE GOLD IN THIS WEDDING BAND—I WON'T WASTE ANOTHER MINUTE—DON'T YOU SEE ALL THESE THINGS MEAN NOTHING TO ME?—YOU CAN HAVE EVERYTHING, BUT I'M TAKING MY HEART WHEN I LEAVE—ALL THE LIES, ALL THE GAMES—ALL THE LONELY NIGHTS WITHOUT YOU—I'VE HAD ENOUGH; I'M CALLING IT QUITS—I'LL BE BETTER OFF WITHOUT YOU—DON'T YOU SEE YOUR APOLOGIES MEAN NOTHING TO ME?—YOU CAN HAVE EVERYTHING, BUT I'M TAKING MY HEART WHEN I LEAVE—THEY SAY YOU CAN'T MAKE A MAN DO WHAT IS RIGHT— BE GOOD TO HIS KIDS AND STAND BY HIS WIFE—SO I'M STARTING OVER NOW THAT I'VE FOUND MY STRENGTH—SAVE ALL YOUR TEARS; YOU DON'T MEAN WHAT YOU SAY—AND YOU CAN'T BELIEVE THE DEVIL ANYWAY

YEAH, YOU CAN'T BELIEVE THE DEVIL ANYWAY— SO, TAKE THE CAR—TAKE THE HOUSE—TAKE THE FURNITURE IN IT—TAKE THE GOLD IN THIS WEDDING BAND—I WON'T WASTE ANOTHER MINUTE—DON'T YOU SEE ALL THESE THINGS MEAN NOTHING TO ME?—YOU CAN HAVE ALL YOUR PRETTY THINGS—BUT I'M TAKING MY HEART WHEN I LEAVE—YEAH, I'M TAKING MY HEART WHEN I LEAVE—I'M TAKING MY HEART WITH ME...

I think that it is obvious the first set of lyrics you just read was about my marvelous first husband. What may not be obvious is why I wrote what I did. My first husband, for some unknown reason, puts high value on what he owns. It is like he is trying to over compensate for a shitty personality and hopes all his pretty things will blind anyone to his true self. When he kicked me out, and during the divorce process, he wasn't about to part with any of his things. It is like he would rather own a piece of furniture or new vehicle than he would want the love of his own children. This is what I kept in mind when I wrote those lyrics. My first husband can keep everything, but my heart does not come with a price tag and can never be owned. I don't think my first husband realizes that not all people can be bought or impressed with what he owns or drives. I wish he'd realize that when it comes to our children. I am trying to teach our children that money and pretty things won't make you happy; unconditional love does. I am not sure my first husband will ever understand that you cannot buy someone's love or loyalty or trust. I don't ever think he'll understand that it isn't what you own that will get you into Heaven. Though, maybe he could care less about things like that.

STARTING HERE, STARTING NOW
by L. A. Burnett

THERE'S SO MANY THINGS I WANNA DO WITH YOU—
STARTING NOW, RIGHT NOW—I WANNA LEAVE THE
PAST BEHIND AND FALL IN LOVE AGAIN—
STARTING NOW, RIGHT NOW—I WANNA WALK OUT
OF THE SHADOWS OF EMPTINESS AND DOUBT—I
WANNA FEEL WHAT HAPPINESS IS ALL ABOUT—
STARTING HERE, STARTING NOW—I WANNA LIVE
FOR THE FIRST TIME—(STARTING HERE, STARTING
NOW)—I WANNA DANCE FOR THE FIRST TIME—
(STARTING HERE, STARTING NOW)—TAKE MY
SHOES OFF; RUN BAREFOOT THROUGH THE RAIN—
LOOK INTO YOUR EYES AND NEVER FEEL
ASHAMED—(STARTING HERE, STARTING NOW)

I WANNA WATCH THE SUNRISE IN THE COMFORT
OF YOUR ARMS—STARTING NOW, RIGHT NOW—I
WANNA MAKE SWEET LOVE TO YOU KNOWING I'M
THE ONLY ONE—STARTING NOW, RIGHT NOW—I
WANNA FEEL MY HEART BEAT FASTER WITH EACH
AND EVERY KISS—I WANNA HEAR MY NAME
WHISPERED SOFTLY ON YOUR LIPS—STARTING
HERE, STARTING NOW—STARTING HERE, STARTING
NOW—STARTING HERE, STARTING NOW—STARTING
NOW…

This was a rough time for me. I know that is an odd thing for me to say, but I don't mean a rough time for me because I was battling with the after effects of abuse. I met my current husband, I instantly fell in love with him, and knew I didn't want to mess things up like my first husband constantly told me I had done with him. I also didn't want to be wrong and find this man was the Bounce Back guy that I would put through Hell during my recovery only to find I made a mistake. I found that he wasn't just the Bounce Back guy and that he wasn't a jerk like my first husband. This man came into my life to help with what was left of me (like I mentioned earlier) and he wasn't about to let me run him off! He fell in love with me, flaws and all. He held me tightly and dried my tears after a long night of bad dreams. He let me have the freedom to make my own decisions and never expected me to be perfect. He found me sexy whether I was wearing his sweats and sweatshirt or I was wearing a short skirt and high heels. I knew I loved him and that I didn't want to let him go. I just needed to get passed some emotional road blocks first that I knew he couldn't help me with. I was so used to being yelled at and not having my own voice that I had no idea how to express all that I felt for this beautiful man. So, what do you do when you can't find your voice? You simply write… And I did.

IF SHE HAD A NAME
by L. A. Burnett

(You ladies are in luck because I actually attempted to type this one properly. I generally write for myself, but wanted my brother to see this last one.)

If she had a name; what was it?—She fell in love with a man that was only a dream—Woke up to find she was suddenly Mrs. So and so—Where did her name go?—If she had a life; where was it?—She spent too much time going out of her mind.—Turned around to find that once was hers now was his.

He controlled it. . .—No more—She was tired of the lies; tired of the pain; tired of the fights—She packed her bags and ran out the door crying, "no more."—And he screamed—"Run all you like! You know you can't hide; all in good time I'll find out just where you've gone—And I'll bring you home."—She prayed, "no more."—If there was freedom; would she ever taste it?—She changed her address; colored her hair, knowing it was only a matter of when and where he'd find her there.—If she had a chance; it now was gone—She was back in the hell she knew all too well—He sat back with a smile and just laughed as she cried—He said, "I told you you were mine"—No more—She was tired of the lies; tired of the pain; tired of the fights—She tried to run, but he already won.—She begged, "no more."—And he screamed, "I told you you could run; I told you you could hide!—But all in good time you knew that I would find you, and I found you."—She cries, "no more."—If there was peace; she found it.—I'm standing here alone; staring at a headstone—Knowing all too well that could be me if I don't break free.—For her I cry, "no more."

It will always choke me up to read that last song of mine. I went through that Hell, other women went through that Hell, YOU are going through that Hell! What gives any human being the right to beat down another? What gives any human being the right to truly believe they can "own" another? What gives any human being the right to rob the person they profess to love of their freedoms? Tell me who died and made all abusers the carriers of the God card. When you are in that Hell, you swear in your heart it will never end; there's no way out... But, there is! Believe me, there is a way out. You are not alone in the fight for freedom, the quest to find the light at the end of the tunnel, or to dream of a day when your life is your own; you're not alone...

I know that this little journey of mine that started just over four and a half years ago is not over. I will have my moments when the ghosts will come back to try to haunt me. I will have my days when the past attempts to camp out at my front door. I will have my moments of weakness when I feel I do not deserve happiness or love. I know though, in my heart, that I am no longer alone. There are hundreds upon hundreds of women, of all ages and backgrounds, that have walked along the same treacherous path to recovery as I have. I pray that my words reach as many of those women as possible and that they realize that they are not alone; not anymore...

EPILOGUE

A few weekends ago I went with my husband up to my aunt and uncle's campsite, near Lake Wentworth, for what I like to call "Soul Recharging". We spent the weekend with my aunt and uncle doing things like fishing, sitting around the campfire, playing dice games, and talking about life, love, and the garbage ex's put others through. It was during one of our late night fishing trips that I realized something that most people take for granted; the stars. Yes, I understand I am blind and therefore cannot see the stars, but I looked Heavenward that evening anyway. In looking up at the night sky, something occurred to me. Shortly after meeting my first husband I stopped looking Heavenward; I stopped looking at the stars. When is the last time any of you ladies sat outside, looked up, and just marveled in the stars? When is the last time you looked at them and either wished, prayed, or dreamt of having something more for yourself as a woman? I think we die a little inside, as abused women, when we stop looking up at the Heavens and merely stare down into Hell each day we crawl out of bed. I suppose that is my opinion though, yes?

I stopped staring down into the pit of Hell the moment I acknowledged I was a victim of domestic violence and decided I wanted to become a survivor. I didn't look Heavenward though. I concentrated on looking ahead to the next minute, then hour, then day, then week; you get the picture. It is a matter of holding our heads high again ladies; holding our heads proud. Once we can do that, we'll all be able to gaze into the night sky and either wish, pray, or dream of a new dawn (a new day) free from all the

LILY ANNE BURNETT

violence, rage, and negativity heaped upon us by our abusers. Something as simple as looking up at the Heavens will make you realize or reinforce the fact that you are not the only woman looking up at those same stars and holding on to the same hope of freedom from abuse.

It was also while I was looking up at the night sky that I realized all things; good or bad; must come to an end and that includes this here book of mine. I don't want to leave you hanging though about some stuff I mentioned here and there throughout the previous pages. I think we all deserve a little closure of some sort, don't you? Hold on a minute… my dryer is beeping for attention. At least I am not jumping off topic to grab a cup of coffee, right? You all know I will be right back…

I'm back… Oh gosh, where to start; hmmm… Well, first off I mentioned here and there about some "female problems" I was having to endure. As of right now they are only worsening. I am going to actually have to look up the spelling of a couple of things and will be right back; sorry. Remember how I went to my primary care physician and all he wanted to do was send me to a shrink and pump me up with , what he referred to as, mood behavior drugs? Also remember how I went to a gynecologist my PCP finally referred me to, but I was determined to get a second opinion? Well, at the end of May I finally got my second opinion and here we go with the results of that… Drum roll please… I have a bladder that is beginning to fall, a rectocele that is getting larger by the day, a slight cystocele caused by the falling bladder that is worsening, and collapsing vaginal walls. Does any of that sound like a "mood behavior drug" would be the cure-all or that a psychiatrist could wave their magic wand and make me better? Didn't think so; stupid primary care physician. So now what? Now I get to wait for a specialist in the field of prolapses that can give me the once over and toss out surgical options. That appointment is one month away. I have my days when it is no big deal to have to wait and I have my days where I cannot handle the discomfort, the pain, the constant trips to the restroom to pee, or the increasing difficulty I am having while trying to be intimate with my husband. Not to mention on those latter days I am a raving bitch to be around! I wouldn't trade what I am going through for anything though because I have three gorgeous children to show for all of it. I can see why ladies nowadays are choosing to have Cesareans though.

Second, I believe I mentioned the head games my children's father is still playing with me and the odds I will have to take him to court soon for contempt. (Deep sigh) I, unfortunately, will have to file court papers with the state of Connecticut next month. My children's father feels he has the right to keep the children from me on my court appointed Saturday to see them because "his vacation is more important"; whatever. This book will be out of my hands by the time any results come back from the whole thing with court, so please just keep me in your thoughts and prayers, as well as my children; thanks. I'll toss in there that I had also said I feel nothing for my once abuser, but that I might feel something by the time I was done with this book. My feelings today? They are the same as they were when I wrote about them earlier; I feel nothing. Understand I feel contempt for his attempts at manipulation, I hate how he uses our children as unknowing pawns in his need to control the universe, and I am annoyed at his lack of concern for being a good example for our children. With all that said (long story short); I can't stand the man's behavior. He, as a human being, still means nothing to me. I also hold in my heart the belief that a person can only walk so long with the Devil before they fall. My first husband's day is coming. No, that is not a threat; it is a fact. There are checks and balances in this world and you can only hurt others for so long before you are knocked down a few pegs…

Third, I talked a bit about my current husband. We have been married for almost two and a half years and I still stand by my feelings that he is, and will always be, my Prince Pretty Damn Close and that he came into my life to help with what was left of me. He is teaching me everyday that love is a good thing, that I do not need to be perfect, that I can say what I am feeling without fear of repercussion, and that I deserve all the blessings life brings my way. My husband is a good man; a true man; a real man. My first husband was none of those things and made me believe that no man could ever be those things. NO MORE! I WILL FEEL THAT WAY NO MORE!!!

Oh, before I forget… I went off about the state of New York's way of nailing out-of-state drivers with speeding tickets. My husband's ticket arrived in the mail a few days ago and the lovely state of New York will be taking my husband for a ride to the tune of $175.00. And who says New York isn't the best place ever to travel through? Get this; and maybe someone will someday give me an answer to this; the ticket was only for $90.00, but then he was nailed a surcharge of $85.00. What the heck is the surcharge of $85.00 for? If my husband was nailed that charge because he is an out-of-state driver; someone needs to give the state of New York the "what for"!

Lastly, I will reiterate what I have been hopefully drilling into your hearts and minds throughout this book; YOU ARE NOT ALONE, not anymore. We abused, and once abused, women make up a significant portion of this world's population. It is time to stand up for what is right; stand up and be counted; stand up for any woman who is no longer with us due to the violence put upon her by another human being. Despite what your abuser or other wretched person around you may say; you deserve happiness, you deserve love, you deserve to live and not just exist. Be the vibrant, intelligent, proud woman you were before all Hell broke loose! Stand up and shine brightly that inner light that your abuser tried so desperately to extinguish…

No more are you alone. No more are you going to feel you are shedding tears alone. No more are you going through endless, sleepless nights alone. No more are you alone on the road to recovery and freedom. No more should you, or any abused woman, feel afraid to reach a hand out for the life line of help. Please be strong; please stand proud; please fight back; please choose to be a survivor of domestic violence and not another victim or statistic. As you already know I am not a fan of repeating affirmations to yourself in the mirror. If that is a path you choose though when you decide to rid yourself of abuse, please add in there the following: "I am not alone; not anymore!"

PS. May any victim of violence truly find peace in their lives. May they choose to live and not merely exist. May they fight for what is right and what is true in this world. May they break the cycle of abuse and know they are not alone as they battle against domestic violence. May they find the inner strength to face another day until they are free from abuse… You're not alone ladies; not anymore!